The making of the education system 1851-81

The making of the education system 1851-81

Donald K. Jones
Lecturer in Education
University of Leicester

Routledge & Kegan Paul
London, Henley and Boston

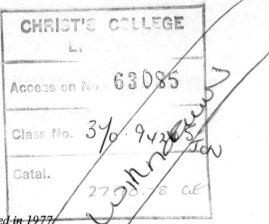
First published in 1977
by Routledge & Kegan Paul Ltd
39 Store Street,
London WC1E 7DD,
Broadway House,
Newtown Road,
Henley-on-Thames,
Oxon RG9 1EN and
9 Park Street,
Boston, Mass. 02108, USA
Set in IBM Press Roman by
Express Litho Service (Oxford)
and printed in Great Britain by
Unwin Brothers Limited
The Gresham Press, Old Woking, Surrey
A member of the Staples Printing Group

British Library Cataloguing in Publication Data

Jones, Donald K

The making of the education system, 1851–81. –
(Students library of education).
1. Education – England – History
I. Title II. Series
370'.942   LA631.7   77–30142

ISBN 0 7100 8707 1

The Students Library of Education has been designed to meet the needs of students of Education at Colleges of Education and at University Institutes and Departments. It will also be valuable for practising teachers and educationists. The series takes full account of the latest developments in teacher-training and of new methods and approaches in education. Separate volumes will provide authoritative and up-to-date accounts of the topics within the major fields of sociology, philosophy and history of education, educational psychology, and method. Care has been taken that specialist topics are treated lucidly and usefully for the non-specialist reader. Altogether, the Students Library of Education will provide a comprehensive introduction and guide to anyone concerned with the study of education, and with educational theory and practice.

Much has been written about the Education Act of 1870, which laid the basis for universal, compulsory, elementary education in England and Wales, but there is no single book which effectively sets this measure in its context, dealing both with its antecedents and its outcome. Mr Jones's work fills that gap.

An important educational measure of this kind is the resultant of a complex play of forces, social, political and economic. It cannot be interpreted purely in educational terms, but requires close study of the variety of factors which led finally to acceptance of the need for government action in this field. In this book, Mr Jones examines closely developments in related fields which bear on this decision, concentrating especially on the political and religious controversies by which it was marked. He also goes beyond the 1870 Act itself to trace subsequent developments which led finally to the imposition of a fully compulsory system throughout the country.

In particular Mr Jones shows that the 1870 Act was no isolated step but, in effect, the last of a series of measures which had as their aim the overall reorganization of educational provision affecting all social classes — measures which were carried through in the period 1850 to 1870.

This book throws light on the politics of education in mid-Victorian England. It enhances understanding of the forces bringing about educational change, and so of the relations between education and society.

BRIAN SIMON

Contents

Contents

Preface

In 1851 England still qualified for Thomas Wyse's description of 1837 as 'the one great exception to the entire civilized world' (Wyse, 1968 ed., p. 62), in that she lacked a national system of education. Education was neither free, compulsory, nor universal, and the question of whether or not to send children to school was considered to be solely for parents to decide. The role of the state was confined to stimulating the educational efforts of voluntary organizations by means of exchequer grants in return for their submission to government inspection of their schools.

Thirty years later, not only had the state become directly responsible for providing universal elementary education through the Elementary Education Act of 1870, but, by means of two further acts of 1876 and 1880, had asserted its right to compel parents to send their children to school.

It is the purpose of this book to provide an account of the reasons for these changes, and to describe how they came about.

I am extremely grateful to Professor Brian Simon not only for his advice and encouragement while the book was in preparation, but also for reading the typescript and for his helpful suggestions.

I also wish to acknowledge the help received from my wife, from Mrs Joan Beardsworth and, in particular, Mrs Audrey Dunning, who typed the manuscript. The responsibility for any faults, however, rests firmly on my shoulders.

DKJ

Abbreviations

The following abbreviations are used in the text:

CCM   Minutes of the Committee of the Privy Council on Education
HC   House of Commons Debates: Third Series
NPSA Minutes   Minutes of the National Public School Association
NPSA Report   Annual Report of the National Public School Association

Chapter one

Education in the year of the Great Exhibition

For the British public the Great Exhibition, which opened in the Crystal Palace on 1 May 1851, was the occasion for self-congratulation and smug satisfaction – sentiments which were distinctly reflected in the Christmas editorial of the *Manchester Guardian* at the end of the year:

> The best contribution that anyone can make to the happiness of the Christmas circle is to show its members that they have good grounds for satisfaction, for hope, and for self approval. We are glad, therefore, to be able to say that English society has never a better right than at the present moment, to sit quietly under a sermon with that pleasing moral. In all our relations, we have at least as much, if not more, substantial reason for contentment and thankfulness, than at the close of any past year in our history (Briggs, 1954, p. 57).

The grounds for congratulation, it appears, were cheap food, clothing, shelter and transport, in reach of all but the destitute, peace both at home and abroad, a prospect of boundless progress and 'an unprecedented growth of good feeling among our widely separated classes'. The writer also discerned improvements in manners and public morals, 'and, in general terms, a patient, but earnest desire of progressive improvement in all ranks of people' (ibid.).

Such complacency was in part justified. If the number of prizes awarded to the British exhibits at the exhibition is taken as a measure, then Britain clearly led the world in technology. Moreover, the greater degree of social cohesion, referred to in the editorial, presaged the advent of the prosperous 'golden years' of the third quarter of the nineteenth century, during the greater part of which Britain was truly the workshop of the world, having no serious industrial rival. It was in these years that the world railway system was laid, largely with British capital and equipment. The coal, iron and steel industries prospered and engineering and chemicals developed as new industries. Moreover,

1

despite the repeal of the Corn Laws in 1846, agriculture enjoyed a twenty-year period of unprecedented prosperity, which was only broken in 1873 when the importation of American cheap grain knocked the bottom out of the British market.

Admittedly there were to be some shocks. The inadequacies in the conduct of the Crimean War, the Indian Mutiny and the Cotton Famine caused anxiety, as also did the financial crisis of 1857 and the crash of the bank of Overend Gurney in 1866. Moreover the 'Sheffield outrages', which helped to promote the setting up of the Royal Commission on the trade unions in 1867, showed that all was not well on the labour front. Nevertheless, these were merely fluctuations in the gradual but continuous trend toward better conditions which characterized the period.

This general movement towards prosperity had an emollient effect on social movements. After the repeal of the Corn Laws in 1846 the effective demand for electoral reform died down, concomitant with a change in the character of working-class movements which became progressively less eager to overturn the capitalist system and instead, like the New Model Unions, of which the Amalgamated Society of Engineers was the prototype, concentrated on exploiting the more immediate advantages within it.

The reaction to the Great Exhibition

Not everybody, however, shared the complacency of the *Manchester Guardian*. To those who were perceptive enough to see it, the threat of American and European industrial competition, clearly manifest by 1881, could be discerned thirty years before at the Crystal Palace. As Richard Cobden, the Sussex-born leader of the Anti-Corn Law League and Lancashire calico-printer, stated in Manchester in December 1851:

> I don't think it is safe for us as a nation to be the most ignorant
> Protestant people on the face of the earth. This is a period in the
> world's history when the very security, the trade, and the progress
> of a nation depend, not so much on the contest of armies, as on the
> rivalry in the science and the arts which must spring from education.
> Did any reflecting man walk through the Great Exhibition without
> feeling that we were apt to be a little under a delusion as to the
> quality of men in other parts of the world, and their capacity to
> create these arts of utility of which we were apt to think sometimes
> we possess a monopoly of production in this country? I don't think
> we can wait (Armytage, 1952, pp. 207–8).

Cobden, in fact, was sounding the tocsin for the growing industrial competitiveness of America, a country which, as will be seen, sent him into paroxysms of admiration. He was joined in his misgivings by the Prince Consort and by Lyon Playfair, Professor of Chemistry at the Royal School of Mines, a commissioner of the Great Exhibition and one of Prince Albert's closest associates. In *Lectures on the Results of the Great Exhibition* (1851), Playfair stressed that the country's natural advantages in the possession of raw materials would have to be supplemented by a more efficient exploitation of her intellectual endowment, a theme which Prince Albert enlarged upon in his message to his fellow commissioners immediately after the exhibition. Britain's natural economic advantages, he considered, had been eroded by improvements in transport and the exploitation of scientific knowledge by her rivals. Crucial to this process was the development in France and Germany of entire systems of technical and scientific education. It was, therefore, 'an obviously growing necessity (that Britain) should afford its manufacturers the means of acquiring that knowledge without which they cannot long keep foremost in the struggle of the nations' (Appleman *et al.*, 1959, p. 104).

In response to these warnings, and encouraged by Prince Albert, the Society of Arts pressed the government to take the initiative in the provision of technical education, the outcome of which was the establishment in 1853 of the Department of Science and Art out of the Council of the School of Design at the Board of Trade. It was this department which, from 1859, under the sway of the former Crimean Officer, J. F. D. Donnelly, the 'very model of a modern major-general' of the *Pirates of Penzance* (Armytage, 1964, p. 121), injected science into the school curriculum by means of a system of payment by results, the number of candidates for examination rising from approximately 1,300 in 1861 to over 100,000 in 1887 (Cardwell, 1972, p. 89).

The question of national efficiency

What worried Cobden, however, was not so much the lack of science teaching in schools, but the fact that in 1851, in contrast to its Continental and American rivals, the most advanced industrial nation in the world was devoid of an articulated system of national elementary education upon which to build a higher educational superstructure. For example, in Prussia the state had taken control of education in order to build a new nation in the aftermath of the traumatic defeat by Napoleon at Jena in 1806. Similarly in post-revolutionary France the victor of Jena centralized the state's control over the educational system in the hope of producing loyal Frenchmen. In the United States the establishment of a State Board of Education in Massachusetts, under the secretaryship of Horace Mann in 1837, signified the growing trend towards bureaucratization in North America. Education had been recognized, particularly in New England, as a vitally important means of social control and cultural preservation from the time of the first settlers, and it became even more so in the second quarter of the nineteenth century under the impact of the triple problem of industrialization, urbanization and Irish immigration (Katz, 1968, p. 6). Scotland, moreover, had possessed rate-supported parochial schools since the seventeenth century, the Dutch, meanwhile, having given Europe her first system of popular education in 1808 (Sturt, 1967, p. 50).

Each of these countries had developed education systems in response to peculiar, and sometimes traumatic, political or religious circumstances. In England, however, in the absence of revolution, enemy occupation, or a religious creed dependent on universal literacy, the traditional post-Reformation method of providing education by voluntary, charitable means, supplemented by a government subsidy for elementary education after 1833, had sufficed. The effect of industrialization, England's equivalent shock, on education is still the subject of debate. It is reasonable to suppose that it ought to have created a demand for a literate labour force to which the state would have responded by establishing a centralized educational system similar to Continental models. Dr Sanderson, however, arguing from the Lancashire evidence, has stated that it produced precisely the opposite effect: education during the initial stages of industrialization was not only irrelevant to industrial change, but suffered a decline in standards, at least at elementary level (Sanderson, 1972, pp. 75–103). Professor Hobsbawm has drawn similar conclusions (Hobsbawm, 1969, pp. 59–60). Professor West, on the other hand, insists that mass, popular education not only experienced expansion during the early phase of the industrial revolution, but that it also played a significant role in the industrialization process (West, 1975, p. 256).

Whatever may be the final outcome of this particular debate, it is clear that the education necessary to produce the clock-makers, instrument-makers, millers, colliery-engineers and other skilled workers required to initiate industrial 'take-off' was available from voluntary, informal, private or other sources, and that state provision did not appear to be necessary (Hartwell, 1971, pp. 226–44). Nevertheless, the doubts about the efficiency of British industry, planted in the minds of prominent individuals by what they saw at the Crystal Palace, created a new situation. Education, in addition to the miscellaneous functions previously assigned to it such as the promotion of social harmony, moral regeneration and the protection of the young, was now assigned the economic function of promoting national prosperity through the creation of an efficient, disciplined and literate labour force. The growing conviction that this was possible, proselytized in particular by Joseph Chamberlain, the Birmingham screw manufacturer, and by

Cobden's hosiery-manufacturing disciple, A. J. Mundella, added a decisively powerful argument to the armoury of those who wanted to establish a national system of education in this country, as will be seen in chapter four.

Social and demographic changes

The question of national efficiency and the efforts to devise educational strategies for its promotion were only symptoms of the wider nineteenth-century problem of coping with a rapidly changing society, characterized by industrialization and population growth. Admittedly the second quarter of the century had witnessed the most rapid and devastating growth of these two forces; nevertheless, as Dr Kitson Clark reminds us (Clark, 1962, 1965 edn, pp. 84ff.), the third quarter was a testing period during which, in England, they were accommodated, mainly because, fortuitously, they happened to coincide: a stroke of good fortune enjoyed neither by contemporary Ireland nor twentieth-century India, where a rapidly increasing population unattended by industrialization proved to be economically disastrous. By 1851 the impact of these two forces was already transforming the role of the state from a minimal to a high level of intervention; a process which has continued to the present day.

If in 1851 the country exhibited many features redolent of the eighteenth century, there is no denying that the intervening thirty-year period down to 1881 was such that the picture at the latter date was very different. For example, although the rate of population growth was less than in the previous quarter, the 17,927,609 people who inhabited England and Wales in 1851 had increased their numbers by half to a total of 25,974,439 by 1881; moreover they found the attraction of the town irresistible. In 1851 the population had only just crossed the Rubicon of urbanization, townsmen outnumbering countrymen for the first time. But the trend was inexorable, and by 1861 the ratio was 5:4. Twenty years later, in 1881, there were twice as many urban as rural dwellers, by which time probably 40 per cent of the population lived in the six growing conurbations of London, south-east Lancashire, the West Midlands, West Yorkshire, Merseyside and Tyneside (Hobsbawm, op. cit., p. 158). Fortunately, the expanding economy was able, by and large, to absorb the extra increment. According to R. Dudley Baxter (1868) capital increased in value between 1855 and 1865 at the rate of £124 million per year, and by a further 40 per cent in the following decade (Giffen, 1889); a spate of investment which reached its never-to-be-exceeded peak in 1872–4 (Ashworth, 1960, pp. 5–7).

The occupational structure meanwhile underwent a shift from manufacturing to service occupations. While domestic service, mainly

5

employing women, increased in number from 900,000 in 1851 to 1·8 millions in 1881 (representing one in seven of the population), agriculture suffered a decline in its share of the labour force from 21 per cent to 11·5 per cent by the latter date, and manufacturing similarly declined from 32·7 to 30·7 per cent. Moreover, within the manufacturing section of industry, textiles, largely becoming a woman's industry, lost men to engineering, ship-building and other metal trades, with the result that the share of the manufacturing population employed by these trades rose from 15 per cent in 1851 to 23 per cent thirty years later; a shift which reflects the demand latterly being made by industry for better educated and more highly-skilled workers.

What agriculture and manufacturing lost, other sectors gained. For example, the number of white-collar workers doubled in the 1860s and again in the 1870s, numbering about 100,000 in 1871 as a result of expansion in merchanting and finance. The railways, meanwhile, gave employment to an army of transport workers, and further expansion took place in the professions. Such proportional changes in the service sector provide an index of the growing sophistication of the economy as well as an indication of the increasing demand for a more literate population throughout the period.

Despite the high rates of economic growth, however, Britain remained a low-consumption economy. According to R. Dudley Baxter, in 1867 over three-quarters of the population were of the 'manual labour class', only 15 per cent of whom, at the most, belonged to the reasonably well paid 'labour aristocracy' earning between 28 shillings and 40 shillings per week. Fifty per cent were either unskilled, female, or agricultural workers earning between 10 and 12 shillings per week, and the rest came somewhere in between. The middle class, meanwhile, numbered no more than 200,000 (Hobsbawm, op. cit., p. 159). For the working classes, except perhaps the labour aristocracy who were well enough organized to provide their own sickness benefits, life could be very precarious indeed. Yet even for skilled workers and the lower echelons of the middle classes, in the absence of any system of social security, the illness or death of the family bread-winner could make the abyss of destitution a constant threat. After all, the death rate only began its steady decline after 1870. Moreover, although these were the 'golden years' of the century, it was only in the late 1860s that real wages began to show a marked rise, after which between 1862 and 1875 they rose by 40 per cent; a trend which permitted an improvement in working-class diet and the production of consumer goods for a working-class clientele (ibid., p. 163).

What is remarkable, in view of such low remuneration in an age of regressive taxation, is the high proportion of the cost of elementary education borne by the working class in the form of school pence, which varied from a quarter to as much as three-fifths of the total

(*Newcastle Report,* i, p.71). Nevertheless, it is hardly surprising, under the circumstances, that the age of compulsory school attendance does not rise beyond ten years during the period in question, although the development of higher tops and higher grade schools after 1870 can be interpreted as a response to increasing affluence and improved job opportunities for those with the requisite skills.

The problem of the city

None of the changes outlined above disturbed mid-Victorian England more than the growth of industrial cities, because their rate of expansion always tended to outstrip the continuous attempts to improve them. Victorian cities inspired both admiration and fear. To Disraeli, Manchester was 'the most wonderful city of modern times'. Only the philosopher could 'conceive the grandeur of Manchester and the immensity of its future' (Briggs, 1963, 1968 edn, p. 63). Others were less euphoric. To Lord Shaftesbury they were places where the masses were 'uninfluenced by, because untouched by, any moral or religious discipline' (ibid.). Moreover, in contrast with hierarchically structured rural communities, where, the Unitarian minister Robert Vaughan explained, 'everyman is known, where all his movements are liable to observation, and the slightest irregularity becomes a matter of local notoriety', the city provided a disconcerting cloak of anonymity, hiding the nefarious activities of the 'ill-disposed' (ibid.). Even more disturbing, as a result of the growth of middle-class suburbs, they were already, by the 1860s, beginning to exhibit to an uncompromising degree the division between social classes in spatial as well as economic terms. Consequently they came to be seen by both Evangelicals and Utilitarians alike as hives of revolutionary activity, populated largely but not exclusively by pauperized, ignorant, ubiquitous, Irish immigrants (Engels, 1845, 1969 edn, pp. 122, 152).

Reflecting on the urban problem in 1846, Joseph Kay, the younger brother of Kay-Shuttleworth, the first Secretary to the Committee of Council on Education, wrote: 'In assembling masses of workmen there are always two special dangers: a low state of intellect, occasioning improvidence, and an absence of religious feeling, producing immorality and insubordination' (Kay, 1846, p. xi). Two years earlier, Frederick Engels had interpreted the same situation in terms of social class formation: 'Without the great cities and their forcing influence upon the popular intelligence, the working class would be far less advanced than it is' (Engels, op. cit., p. 152). However, while the latter merely awaited the advent of the dictatorship of the proletariat, the former urged the state to take countervailing measures; the state-supported school must be intruded into the city in order to inculcate habits of morality, religion and providence among the urban poor.

As these comments clearly illustrate, the city, with its concentration of filth, misery, vice, crime and political volatility, posed a potential threat to the social order to which few could remain indifferent. Its effect was to focus attention upon, and to present as utterly intolerable, abuses which in previous generations had been virtually unnoticed. Moreover, the city illustrated with uncompromising clarity the failure of voluntary, pre-industrial *laissez-faire* methods to cope with contemporary urban problems, the magnitude of which was unprecedented. Consequently, as will be seen, the alleged failure of the voluntary schools to reach a large section of the urban poor provided a second, very powerful, argument in support of a collectivist solution to the problem of providing universal elementary education.

Government growth and education

Loudly though Cobden might deplore the educational state of the English in 1851, this country was by no means devoid of schools. As might be expected, however, existing provision clearly reflected the prevailing social structure. The nine great public schools, together with a number of prestigious grammar and proprietary schools which were soon to rank alongside them, served the aristocracy, the gentry and the upper middle classes. The bulk of the middle classes were catered for by endowed grammar schools and numerous proprietary and private schools, while elementary schools, both voluntary and endowed, some of which were in receipt of government grants and others of a private venture nature which did not qualify for government inspection and state-aid, served the section of the working classes who could afford to pay the weekly fees of two pence and five pence. By 1851, the components of this framework of provision, for it can scarcely be called a system, were already causing anxiety, and were soon to be investigated by a series of Royal Commissions, two of which had begun to examine the universities of Oxford and Cambridge in the previous year.

It was the education of the most potentially volatile section of the community, the working classes, however, which caused the greatest anxiety. Hence the increasing involvement of the state in assisting the educational efforts of voluntary societies after 1833. For this reason, nineteenth-century developments in elementary education are as much concerned with government growth as with teaching children. As Professor Taylor has stated: 'The governments of early and mid-Victorian England did not so much seek to provide new remedies for old problems as to come to terms with the new crises which accompanied a rapidly changing social order' (Taylor, 1972, p. 56). It was in response to such crises that the 'legislative-cum-administrative' process of government expansion, as illustrated by Professor MacDonagh's model, was set in motion (MacDonagh, 1958, pp. 52–67); a process generally fraught with difficulty, and particularly so in the sphere of education.

Successive attempts in the aftermath of the Napoleonic wars to mitigate what MacDonagh terms an 'intolerable social evil', in this case educational destitution among the poor, had led in 1833 to the voting of the government grant of £20,000 in support of the two main voluntary societies, the National Society and the British and Foreign School Society. Tentative though this financial initiative was, it turned out to be the thin end of the wedge of state intervention, for 'from that point the question was not whether there should be intervention, but what form that intervention should take and how extensive it should be' (Taylor, op. cit., p. 48). Initially it appeared that it would not be extensive, for in spite of Radical demands for a centralized bureaucratic structure on Prussian lines, the voluntary societies, as Lord John Russell explained, already occupied the ground (HC, 45, 275). Consequently, in 1839 the Whig government was content merely to establish a Committee of the Privy Council on Education for the purpose of allocating the government grant. Thus, in common with many other departments, the embryo Department of Education and Science began its existence under the umbrella of the Privy Council.

Immediately it ran into the kind of sectarian difficulty which was to hinder direct state intervention in education until 1870. The problem arose out of the attempt by the Church to reassert its claim to monopolize the education of the nation's poor, and the denial of this claim by the new militant Nonconformist movement, whose main objective under the leadership of the Congregationalist, Edward Miall, was nothing less than the disestablishment of the Church.

The outcome was a series of rebuffs for the state, including the abandonment of a projected undenominational government teacher-training college, the granting of concessions to the voluntary bodies in the choice of HMIs, and the formation of the Voluntaryist party by Congregationalists and Baptists in protest against the pro-Anglican educational clauses of Sir James Graham's factory bill of 1843. Led by Edward Baines, editor of the *Leeds Mercury*, and Edward Miall, this new pressure group withdrew its schools from the orbit of the state by refusing both inspection and the government grant, thereby effectively dividing the Nonconformists on the education issue until Baines's recantation in 1867. Meanwhile, their suspicions that state education meant an Anglican monopoly were in no way relieved by the Church's success in cornering 80 per cent of all exchequer grants for its schools between 1839 and 1850 (Sutherland, 1971, p. 16).

Under these circumstances the government was obliged to admit that further progress could only be made through the voluntary societies. With this object in view, Kay-Shuttleworth, Secretary to the Committee of Council on Education in the first ten years of its existence, devised under the Minutes of Council of 1846 the complex system of grants which not only laid the foundations of the elementary teaching profession, but at the same time created the conditions whereby the state inevitably increased its financial stake in elementary education. The result was that by 1860 the education department possessed one of the largest staffs in the Home Civil Service (Hurt, 1971, p. 12), thus giving rise to fears of over-centralization and bureaucratic tyranny, as will be seen in chapter three.

Nevertheless, this policy was a recognition of defeat for the state, for it not only increased the vested interests of the voluntary bodies, particularly the Anglicans, in the status quo, but as Kay-Shuttleworth told the Newcastle Commission, it immeasurably increased the difficulty of supplementing the exchequer grant with a local rate in support of elementary education; a potential source of finance which many school promoters considered to be essential if the objective of providing elementary education for every child was to have the remotest chance of realization (*Newcastle Report,* i, p. 21).

The crisis in the voluntary system

The Minutes of Council of 1846 appeared at a time of growing concern for the state of elementary education. In that year, Horace Mann, the highly respected Secretary to the Massachusetts Board of Education, complained in his *Report of an Educational Tour* (1844), that 'England is the only one among the nations of Europe, conspicuous for its civilization and resources, which has not, and never has had, any system of education for its people' (Smith, 1931, p. 200). His praise for the Prussian schools which he had visited, in contrast, was unstinting.

Meanwhile, in his published letter 'On the means of rendering more efficient the education of the people' (1846), Dean Hook, the High Church Vicar of Leeds, facing the problem of educational destitution in a growing industrial city, urged the state to take over the whole responsibility for secular instruction, leaving religious education to parsons.

It was the Inspectorate, however, which provided the most insistent demand for a major educational initiative. Reporting in 1850 on the desperate financial predicament of schools and the growing impatience of their promoters in the north-west, HMI W. J. Kennedy wrote: 'Men's minds seem more prepared than ever before, nay even anxious, for some great development of the meagre and tantalizing state of popular education. It is felt that very much effort is made for a small result' (CCM, 1850–1, p. 573). The clergy were obliged to enact the part of 'mendicant friars' in order to keep schools in existence, while school managers considered the voluntary system to be a mere stop-gap. He therefore urged the government seriously to consider the bill of the Manchester and Salford Committee on Education which, as will be seen in the next chapter, aimed to provide a local rate in support of voluntary education.

Meanwhile, Kennedy's colleague in the north-east, the Rev. F. Watkins, complained of the 'mockery of education' that only 5 per cent of working-class children stayed on at school long enough to learn something useful, all the 'partial restoratives (having) failed to touch the disease' (ibid., pp. 255–6). His proposed interventionist solution is typical of the response of the new professional bureaucrats to social problems, amounting to an assault on the prevalent *laissez-faire* principle that the individual had an inalienable right to decide whether or not to educate his children. If parents would not forego children's wages and employers deny themselves cheap labour, urged Kennedy, they must be coerced by the law; an argument clearly illustrative of the gradual erosion of *laissez-faire* ideology during the nineteenth century under the impact of immense social problems.

As the following extract shows, Kennedy, like many of his colleagues, thoroughly approved of the government's right to interfere in the lives of individuals in the interests of the community at large. Moreover, he was not given to mincing words:

> I believe, my lords, that most men are growing rather weary of this cuckoo-cry of 'interference', this air-bubble which has nothing but a specious outside. Every law is an interference with the freedom of the subject for the *good* of the subject. The few are restrained that the many may be benefitted. The law which commits the thief to prison is a decided interference with his freedom. And, fortunately for the country, there are many similar instances of stringent interference with the freedom of the subject (ibid.).

The duty of the state, therefore, was to intervene in order to secure for the 'hundreds of thousands of young children in this country condemned to premature labour . . . the freedom of two or three years, that they may be fitted for their work in life' (ibid.).

The Census of 1851

It may be that the HMIs, anxious like all bureaucrats to ensure their own continued existence, exaggerated the deficiencies of popular education, as Professor West suggests (West, op. cit., p. 98). On the other hand, the pressure for state control of education may be interpreted as the desire of a dominant social group to control the socialization of a subordinate group, an interpretation popularized recently by American historians (Katz, 1968, p. 112; 1971, pp. 108–9). There is possibly some truth in both of these interpretations. However, it cannot be denied that the urban problem and others with it, to which Professor West gives scant regard, were traumatic enough to persuade churchmen such as Dean Hook, secular Radicals like Cobden, and professional government servants such as Watkins and Kennedy, to seek a more thoroughly bureaucratic solution to the provision of education than the subsidized voluntary system would permit. Moreover, the educational census which was part of the general census of 1851 provided them with a powerful statistical weapon with which to fight their campaign. It revealed that 2,144,378 children, or 1 in 8·36 of the population, attended day school. Yet it was calculated that three millions should have been at school. Consequently, one million were unaccounted for, being neither at school nor at work. It may be that, as Professor West suggests, the census findings exaggerated the deficiencies of the voluntary system (ibid., pp. 22–9); nevertheless, the important point is that contemporaries found them convincing enough and used them to support their arguments in favour of a national system of education.

If, in the euphoric aftermath of the Great Exhibition, the editor of the *Manchester Guardian* could write complacently about the nation's 'reason for contentment', it is clear that more percipient observers could not share his view. In spite of the country's arrival on the threshold of the prosperous mid-Victorian 'golden era', the problems attendant upon industrialization, population growth, foreign competition and, above all, urbanization, which were clearly visible in 1851, increased rather than diminished during the succeeding thirty years. The very need to cope with these problems had the effect of revolutionizing the role of the state with regard to the individual; a process which is clearly illustrated by the development of national education in the period covered in this book.

Chapter two

The campaign for national education in the 1850s

By the time of Kay-Shuttleworth's premature retirement in 1849 the state was already deeply involved in the provision of elementary education. This was itself a manifestation of the gradual movement towards collectivism which characterized governmental development in England during the nineteenth century. Once it had been admitted that grants would be forthcoming to all applicants who satisfied certain minimum conditions, the degree of state involvement in education depended upon the voluntary activity of individuals and organizations over whom there was little control. As this continued to increase, so, in proportion, did the state's financial involvement in the schools, until in 1870 its role was transformed from stimulating the efforts of others to assuming the responsibility for ensuring the provision of universal elementary education.

Yet there was considerable disagreement as to the desirability of state intervention. The Voluntaryists completely opposed it to the extent of refusing to take advantage of the exchequer grants. The Anglicans, on the other hand, whose organization and efforts had secured for them the bulk of the government grant since 1833, were, understandably, satisfied. Some other groups, however, both Secularist and Denominationalist, whose activities will be described in this chapter, considered that intervention by the state should be far more extensive.

The reason for this view was the evident failure of the voluntary system to reach a considerable section of the population, particularly in the growing industrial towns. Horace Mann's educational census of 1851, *Education in Great Britain*, provided statistical evidence for this defect, but his survey was only available in 1854. Not that it required a census to reveal the enormity of the problem of educational destitution. As Joseph Kay pointed out, the problem was there for all to see:

Independently of any statistics, if you go at any hour into the

13

crowded streets of London, Liverpool, Manchester, Newcastle, Birmingham or any other great town, you will see numbers of young children of both sexes, from four to fifteen years of age, filthy, wretchedly clothed, rude in manners and language, and exhibiting all the signs of poverty, neglect and degradation (Smith, 1931, p. 221).

W. J. Fox's bill

It is not surprising, therefore, to find an early initiative coming from one who was not only well versed in the intricacies of the education question, but who also had first-hand experience of the violence of the urban populace. This was William Johnson Fox, former Unitarian minister of South Place Chapel, Finsbury, Anti-Corn Law League orator and, since 1847, MP for Oldham. His election campaign had been a classic example of pre-ballot electoral violence and corruption. On one occasion he and his son had been obliged to take refuge under their beds in order to protect themselves from the brick-bats with which the hostile crowd bombarded their Oldham hotel.

In 1850 Fox independently introduced an education bill into Parliament proposing to establish a system of national education in England and Wales. This was the first of a series of bills in the post-Corn Law repeal period which attempted to solve the problem of educational destitution, either by supplementing the existing system or completely replacing it. In his speech (HC, 109, 27), he stressed the inadequacy of the voluntary system to embrace the very poor, and urged the need for a more comprehensive measure. He proposed that deficiencies in school accommodation in parishes should be ascertained by HMIs, and the localities invited to remedy these by means of a local rate. Provision was to be made for voluntary school managers not only to share in the existing rate but also to continue to erect denominational schools. The most important provision was that rate support was only to be granted for 'efficient' secular instruction. No financial aid was to be made available for religious instruction. A further proposal provided for the Privy Council to coerce negligent areas into building new schools which would be secular, but in which religious instruction would be given at certain times for children whose parents desired it. The bill is particularly interesting in that it foreshadows both Lowe's Revised Code and Forster's Elementary Education Act by on the one hand demanding a test of efficiency before making a grant, and on the other by attempting to 'fill the gaps' left by the voluntary system.

The champions of the Church were quick to see the proposals as a threat to their near monopoly of elementary education. Sir Robert Inglis, 'the member for Heaven' as he was known, on account of his zealous support of the Church, accused Fox of neglecting the eternal destinies of the children and raised the cry of 'religion in danger', which was to be heard all too frequently in the next two decades. Lord Arundel waxed even more dramatic: 'The two armies were drawing up their forces and the battle was now between religion and irreligion, the Church and Infidelity, God and the Devil, and the reward for which they must contend was Heaven or Hell' (Adams, 1882, p. 154).

On the other hand, A. J. Roebuck, author of the national education scheme of 1833, defended the measure with the familiar Victorian argument, hardly supported by the available evidence, that education had a crime preventative function:

> You make laws, you erect prisons, you have the gibbet, you circulate throughout the country an army of judges and barristers to enforce the law, but your religious bigotry precludes the chance or the hope of your being able to teach the people, so as to prevent the crime which you send round this army to punish (ibid., p. 154).

Fox's motion, defeated by 287 votes to 58, was only the first of a series of attempts in the 1850s to provide rate-supported schools which the children of all denominations would be able to attend, and thereby help to break the sectarian deadlock. The momentum was maintained by a Radical middle-class pressure group based in Manchester, of which Fox had become a member in 1848. It was from this organization and its denominational rivals in the same city that the main impetus towards national education came during the next few years, with the result that 'Manchester led the national debate on education during the 1850s and 1860s, out of which finally came the Education Act of 1870' (Read, 1964, p. 169).

Education and the Free Trade faction

Manchester in mid-century was the undisputed home of successful Radicalism as a result of the success of the Anti-Corn Law League, the pressure group of the rising provincial class of manufacturers. The League's actual achievement was exaggerated by contemporaries, for not only did Corn Law repeal fit logically into Peel's programme of fiscal reform (Clark, 1967, p. 36), but the elements also obliged in tipping the climatic scales in its favour by inducing an Irish famine. Nevertheless, feeding their confidence on this legend and on the superb organizational machinery which the League had built up in Manchester, former free-traders began to seek out new fields to conquer. John Bright, the great League orator, who had worked with Richard Cobden for national education in the 1830s (Read, 1967, p. 76), devoted himself after 1846 to extending the suffrage, believing, correctly as it turned out, that national education was not a suitable programme behind which to unite the Radicals. In contrast his brother, Jacob Bright, and brother-in-law Samuel Lucas, supported by a locally influential group of their former League colleagues, centred on the Presbyterian Church of the Rev. William McKerrow in Lloyd Street, Manchester, embraced the elementary education problem.

Beginning their activities in 1847 they founded the Lancashire Public School Association (LPSA), which in 1850, on becoming a national pressure group, was renamed the National Public School Association (NPSA). They aimed to set up an elaborate scheme of national, free, secular, rate-supported, locally controlled education explicitly based upon the model of the American Common School system as reformed by Horace Mann, Secretary to the Massachusetts Board of Education (not to be confused with the compiler of the educational census).

There is little doubt that one of the motives of the two English Quakers and seven Scottish dissenters who founded the LPSA was to strike a blow at the Anglican Church by breaking its hold on elementary education. The anti-clerical nature of the Anti-Corn Law League had proved congenial to them for similar reasons. There were, however, more specific motives. One of these was the fear of an extension of the franchise to the uneducated proletariat. As one LPSA member's wife wrote: 'If Demos was to be King, then Demos must go to school and be trained to make the best use of his power' (Mills, 1899, p. 153).

Industrial competitiveness was another motive implying that a national education system would send forth a steady stream of inventive geniuses of the calibre of Richard Arkwright, Robert Fulton and James Watt (LPSA, 1850, pp. 91−112).

Their greatest preoccupation, however, was with children of the kind referred to by Joseph Kay who were untouched by the voluntary system. In Manchester alone there were 30,000 children between the ages of three and fifteen who went neither to school nor to work, Sir John Pakington told the House of Commons in 1855 (HC, 137, 649). Consequently, much was made of the incongruity of an education system which subsidized fee-paying parents and gave free education to paupers, but which completely ignored the whole stratum of the population in between, 'from whom the criminal classes spring'. For such children the existing schools were unsuitable, as Dr McKerrow explained to Lord John Russell in 1853 on the occasion of a NPSA deputation to persuade him to adopt the Association's secular plan: 'The Church and Chapel schools are too respectable, are attended by a class of children whose parents would not allow the lower classes to be under the same roof or in the same playground with them' (NPSA Minutes, 6 June 1853).

What was needed, urged the LPSA, was a free secular system of education which would cater not only for children who were attached to religious denominations, but also those whom they failed to reach, without fear of violating the conscience of anyone. This would cost money and the proposals for providing the necessary funds give further insights into the minds of the Victorian provincial Liberal-Radical middle-classes.

It could be argued that it would have been possible to secure an extension of the education system with the aid of central government funds, but in an age which was distrustful of the power of central governments this would have been a most unpopular method. The alternative was to raise the extra funds by a local rate, the effect of which would be to put its deployment into the hands of locally-elected bodies, thereby satisfying aspirations of local democracy and, equally important since the Municipal Reform Act of 1835, civic pride. As Absalom Watkin, a prominent Manchester citizen and NPSA member explained to Lord John Russell in 1853:

> We object to all centralization as dangerous to civil liberty and at variance with constitutional principles. We think that we ought to have the management of our own money and be allowed to supply it for purposes of education, as a majority of the rate-payers may decide (ibid.).

Consequently, within the movement for national education can be seen the growing sense of municipal pride and independence. Not only was this spirit to be manifested in the building of elaborate town halls, but equally, after the 1870 Act, by the construction of palatial board schools. As Francis Adams, the historian of the secularist movement in education, wrote in his *History of the Elementary School Contest in England* (1882): 'The efforts for the separation of schools from the control of the religious communions were partly owing to the growth of the municipal sentiment' (Adams, op. cit., p. 157).

Once the need for a local rate was accepted, it was possible to make a strong case for a secular system, for a denominational rate-supported system would, in the majority of cases, involve the subsidizing of the Anglican schools by Nonconformists; an unacceptable situation. Consequently, although the need for rate aid had become manifest by 1850, it was only in 1870 that an acceptable formula was found. Even then its application was confined to state schools. The voluntary schools had to wait until 1902 for similar assistance.

Cobden and the American Common School System

It was on account of such reasoning that the LPSA chose to adopt the democratically-based Massachusetts system rather than the centralized

17

systems of Prussia and France as its model. In *A Plan for the Establishment of a General System of Secular Education in the County of Lancaster*, published in 1847, Samuel Lucas, the association's prime mover, explained how it was hoped to set up a system of schools, at first in Lancashire, managed and supported with the aid of a rate by local committees and supervised by a county board, as in Massachusetts. One difference between the American system and the proposed Lancashire scheme was that the district committees in Massachusetts had the right to choose whether or not to allow the use of the Bible in schools, but owing to the more complex religious situation in England the LPSA decided that in order to enable all sects to attend the schools the Bible would have to be excluded. As will be seen, this attempt to avoid controversy only resulted in creating it to a greater extent.

Throughout the middle years of the nineteenth century the American common school enjoyed something of a vogue in this country among secular educationists (Farrar, 1965, pp. 36–47). What attracted them, besides its democratic structure, was the unsectarian religious teaching encouraged by Horace Mann in accordance with his general policy on the teaching of religion. He defined this in his Seventh Report: 'Our aim obviously is to secure so much of religious instruction as is compatible with religious freedom', and it was this definition which the LPSA adopted as its own policy (LPSA, *Plan*, 7).

Few people sang the praises of the Massachusetts school louder than George Combe, the Scottish phrenologist, convinced secular educationist and friend of Horace Mann (Grant, 1968, pp. 308–17), and it was from him that Samuel Lucas received the information on which to base the Plan. Another admirer was Richard Cobden who, on a visit to America in 1835, became so ecstatic about the common schools that he determined to transplant them in England, where he hoped they would be agencies for social regeneration:

> Oh happy sight, pregnant with hopes of the character of future generations, I hereby dedicate myself to promoting the cause of the infant school in England where they may become an instrument for ameliorating the fate of the children working in the factories, whose case, I fear, is beyond the reach of all other remedies (Cawley, 1952, p. 121).

Not only the schools but the whole country captivated him, as it did many of his contemporaries such as Harriet Martineau, the political economist, and Sir Charles Lyell, the geologist. He saw it as the 'Utopia of the under-privileged' (Armytage, 1957, p. 301). More ominously, some sixteen years before the warning signs of overseas competition appeared at the Great Exhibition, he had already concluded that the threat to British economic supremacy would come, not from Russia, but from the United States (ibid., p. 302). Of even greater importance was his conviction that the cause of America's prosperity was her system of education. Although, on his return to England, Cobden briefly became involved in Manchester, with the attempt to promote cooperation among the warring religious sects in the provision of elementary education, it was only in 1848, when he had recovered from the exhausting League campaign, that he was able, as he put it, 'to put on my armour for another seven years' war' (Cawley, op. cit., p. 26).

Meanwhile the LPSA had grown rapidly in support and organization, and Samuel Lucas was beginning to think in terms of a national movement employing all the techniques developed by the League on behalf of the LPSA programme. All that was needed was a national leader. Cobden supplied this need when he assumed the leadership of the National Public School Association, the successor to the LPSA which was brought into existence at a great public meeting held in Manchester on 30 October 1850.

The National Conference of the National Public School Association

Supporters of national education from all over the country attended this conference, and the debate which took place sheds much light on current educational problems, and on the religious issue in particular. The delegate from Bradford is of particular interest, being none other than W. E. Forster, not yet elected to Parliament, but revealing already the train of thought which eventually led him to his compromise measure of 1870. He was soon embroiled in a debate which exposed the difficulties of the extreme secularist position.

From the beginning Cobden stressed the need to broaden the basis of support for the new national body. For this reason both he and Forster opposed the suggestion that it should be named 'The National Secular School Association', on the grounds that the word 'Secular' would expose the NPSA to the charge of irreligion. Forster went so far as to threaten to leave the movement if the name was not changed. Cobden, revealing his awareness of the impossibility of success without a united Radical party behind him, made it clear that he was determined to placate Edward Baines and the Voluntaryists in the hope of uniting the whole body of dissent behind the national education movement. Ultimately a consensus was achieved, and the word 'public' was substituted for 'secular'. Further difficulty arose over the use of the Bible. Cobden was adamant that the decision whether or not to use it as a school book should lie not with any central authority but, as in Massachusetts, with the local communities, for the following reasons:

19

> One half of our parishes in the United Kingdom, and a great deal more, are simply rural parishes, containing a few hundred inhabitants. In many cases there is but a parish church, and there is not a Dissenter. Now, I don't understand this to be a plan which should prevent a community like that, where all are agreed, from having the whole bible if they please introduced into their schools (Salis Schwabe, 1895, p. 129).

Nevertheless, bearing in mind the thousands of Irish immigrants in the country, he went on: 'We will not compel the reading of the bible when that shall have the effect probably of deterring Roman Catholics or others from sending their children to the schools' (ibid.).

In short, Cobden's main priority was the establishment of a system of universal elementary education, and he believed that the implementation of the American system, by avoiding sectarian difficulties, provided the only means of achieving his objective. An Anglican himself, he was not interested in Secularism except as a means to an end.

These opinions displeased the convinced Secularists, and one in particular, Dr W. B. Hodgson, an LPSA founder member, a future Assistant Newcastle Commissioner and eventual Professor of Political Economy at Edinburgh, gradually withdrew from the movement. Nevertheless, although a compromise was eventually reached without specifically excluding the Bible from the proposed schools, the following basis was intended to have precisely that effect (Maltby, 1918, p. 81).

> The National Public School Association has for its aim the establishment by law, in such parts of England and Wales as may need them, of Free Schools; which, supported by local committees specially elected for that purpose by the rate-payers, shall impart secular instruction only, leaving to parents and guardians and religious teachers, the inculcation of doctrinal religion to afford opportunities, for which purpose the schools shall be closed at stated times each week (NPSA Minutes, 4 January 1850).

The important point here is that doctrinal religious teaching was to be separated completely from secular instruction and to be taught by people other than the teachers of secular subjects.

Agreement having been achieved, the association's executive committee set about drawing up an education bill and giving some reality to its national aspirations by extending official recognition to representatives in other towns; for example, William Biggs in Leicester, James Hole in Leeds, and William Harris in Birmingham.

The Manchester and Salford Committee on Education

Although a consensus had been reached within the NPSA its difficulties were only beginning, for it was inevitable that its very existence would arouse the opposition of the Denominationalists. Some indication of the nature of this opposition is provided in a letter from the recently retired, yet publicly active, Kay-Shuttleworth, written in reply to an invitation to attend the national conference of the NPSA and published in the *Manchester Guardian* of 6 November 1850. It expresses the anxiety of many people who, although conscious of the need for a sound education system, were also desirous of retaining religious doctrinal teaching in schools. It also reveals his own conviction that the political socialization of the electorate ought to be a prime function of education. The NPSA, he stated, was the 'representative of a great political party', bringing into relief the 'political objects which are dependent on a system of National Education'. These were to ensure to every parent the means of raising his child 'to the exercise of the political franchise with advantage to the State'. So far he was in agreement with the Association's aims. What he could not reconcile himself to was the separation of schools from 'the superintendence of the great religious bodies' and to a system 'in which the religious influence shall not pervade the whole discipline and instruction' (*Manchester Guardian*, 6 November 1850). He concluded with the hope, soon to be realized, that the NPSA before long would subordinate its secular demands in the interests of promoting an acceptable national system. These opinions were shared by W. E. Forster, whose reservations at the national conference are explained in the following letter to Kay-Shuttleworth:

> I do not profess myself a 'Secular', having merely enrolled myself under their flag because there was no other hoisted, and I confess that my object is simply a local rate.... I shall be most happy to press on this new plan as much as I can, though it will need care not to stultify myself by appearing to support two distinct and somewhat opposing plans at once (Smith, 1923, p. 235).

The 'new plan' to which Forster referred had been devised by another pressure group, the Manchester and Salford Committee on Education, which, within two months of Kay-Shuttleworth's letter to the *Manchester Guardian*, had sprung into existence in response to the NPSA's secularist proposals. Politically a mainly Tory-Anglican organization, it boasted the support of the militant Rev. Hugh Stowell, the more moderate Canon Charles Richson of Manchester Cathedral, a number of prominent lay Anglicans, and also some leading Dissenters (Maltby, op. cit., pp. 83–94). Significantly, Kay-Shuttleworth joined its executive committee. The new organization quickly produced a denominational education bill embodying the principles of local control, local rating, free education, the establishment where needed of new schools, and the admission of all children irrespective of their religious beliefs. Lessons in doctrinal religion were, therefore, to be part of the curriculum, but it was envisaged that any difficulties would be avoided by providing schools for all denominations.

Despite Cobden's criticism that it was 'a proposal by which everybody shall be called upon to pay for the religious teaching of everybody else' (ibid., p. 84), the two sides were remarkably close to an agreement. This potentially happy state of affairs was reached when, at a conference in June 1851, the NPSA provided for admission of existing voluntary schools into its scheme as a result of the unsuccessful introduction of the NPSA's Free Schools Bill into Parliament by W. J. Fox earlier in the year.

Much to Kay-Shuttleworth's disappointment, this basis for a compromise was destroyed by the adoption of a resolution, on the instigation of William Entwistle, chairman of the Denominationalist committee and former opponent of the Anti-Corn Law League candidate in the South Lancashire election of 1844, demanding that the Bible should be read in all rate-supported schools. This obtuse manoeuvre gave the already lukewarm Catholics their opportunity to withdraw, and occasioned a warning from Kay-Shuttleworth that without the utmost toleration there could be no hope of success. For the moment his cherished hope of a powerful multi-denominational educational pressure group in the north-west seemed to be more remote than ever.

The Select Committee on Manchester and Salford Education

Meanwhile, the two pressure groups proceeded to nullify each other's efforts. The Manchester and Salford Committee pressed on alone with its Bill, which reached its second reading on 25 February 1852. But there it stopped, when Thomas Milner Gibson, MP for Manchester and a vice-president of the NPSA, successfully moved the appointment of a Select Committee to enquire into the state of education in Manchester and Salford (HC, 119, 1198), on the grounds that Manchester town council had not approved the scheme and that the Salford Council had accepted it only narrowly. Immediately both Manchester organizations indulged in the fashionable Victorian pursuit of collecting statistical evidence in support of their respective cases for presentation to the committee, which began its work on 7 March 1852.

The outcome was remarkable for the insistence by both the Secularists and Denominationalists that, without a system of free, rate-supported education, the task of getting the uneducated and unemployed children into the schools would be impossible. As one might expect, Edward Baines, for the Voluntaryists, was confident that the problem could be solved by voluntary means; a position which he maintained until 1867. He was supported among others by C. H. Hinton, a Baptist minister and a confirmed Voluntaryist, who, noting that 'parliamentary Blue Books are rather like graves in which the most precious things may be buried, than mines out of which the people at large will take the trouble to dig them' (Hinton, 1854, vol. ii, p. 3), took it upon himself to review the evidence in a pamphlet entitled *The Case of the Manchester Educationists*. Hinton disagreed with the conclusions drawn by the two pressure groups. He told Milner Gibson, the committee chairman, that despite the existence of national education systems in other countries 'our educational system must be our own', on account of the peculiar religious situation in Britain. 'And what, in your opinion, must it be?' asked Milner Gibson. 'It must be the voluntary system,' replied Hinton. 'My conviction is that no other will be found practicable in this country' (ibid., p. 98).

There the matter remained for, despite the vast amount of evidence taken, so diverse was the constitution of the committee that it could only agree 'that the Evidence be reported, without any opinion thereon, to the House' (ibid., p. 2). This, stated Hinton, was a 'lame and impotent conclusion', advertising the confused Parliamentary situation on education, the nature of which he described as follows:

> Such are the diversities of opinion which exist among educational
> philanthropists themselves, and the small degree of progress made in
> settling the primary elements of the problem, that upon no one
> point could thirteen men, picked out for the purpose from the
> whole House of Commons, find their way to an agreement. So much
> for the possibilities of educational legislation in England (ibid., p. 3).

So much indeed, for in 1854, the year of publication of Hinton's pamphlet, the Crimean War broke out, forcing 'reform into the background and Palmerston into the foreground' (Maccoby, 1935, p. 323).

The cemetery for defunct Education Bills

One of the reasons for the desultory activity of the Select Committee in 1853 had been the expectation of a government initiative on education. This turned out to be Lord John Russell's Borough Bill of the same year. Drawn up with advice from Kay-Shuttleworth (Smith, 1923, p. 246), it was yet another attempt to secure rate aid for urban schools. However, the proposal to subsidize the voluntary schools by a rate of 6d. in the pound without extending management control to rate payers was unacceptable, and the government let the measure drop. The Manchester and Salford Committee petitioned against the Bill and the NPSA sent a large deputation to Russell to ask him to adopt the Free Schools Bill; a request which he declined. Nevertheless, two positive measures were achieved, one national and the other local. In 1853, as part of Russell's original scheme, a capitation grant was made to inspected rural schools, and three years later similar aid was extended to urban schools. Consequently, the government's financial involvement in education was once again augmented, causing the unease of MPs to grow in proportion to the ever-increasing size of the government grant. These misgivings, which were reflected later in the deliberations of the Newcastle Commission, were partly shared by Kay-Shuttleworth. He approved of the grant to rural schools, but feared that its extension to the towns would stifle the voluntary effort and increase the influence of the central authority: 'A purely centralized administration, if it be not combined with local organization which has its own sphere of action, might paralyse that local activity which is the life of our social organization' (ibid.). Nevertheless, the extent of state involvement continued to increase.

The local repercussion of Russell's bill arose from his remark to the NPSA delegation that they had not 'sufficiently practicalized' their scheme to convince him of its feasibility. The result was the foundation, in 1854, of the Manchester Model Secular School (later named the Manchester Free School) as a prototype of the schools proposed by the NPSA. For thirty-three years this school gave a completely free and efficient secular education to boys of all denominations, including Catholics, from the social class which the NPSA were most concerned to educate, becoming in the process something of a show place (Jones, 1967, pp. 22–33).

Meanwhile, despite the distracting nature of the Crimean War, the flow of education bills into Parliament continued unabated: For example, in 1855 no fewer than five, two of which were Scottish, were introduced. Owing to the unstable Parliamentary situation they were all unsuccessful, but the bill of Sir John Pakington, the Tory member for Droitwich, based on the Manchester and Salford bill which had again been unsuccessful in the previous year, reached a second reading. Pakington was far in advance of the majority of his Tory colleagues on the education question. He was disturbed by the urban problem, and convinced of the inadequacy of the voluntary system to solve it without rate support. On introducing his bill he told the Commons, 'We cannot go on as we are. The voluntary system has broken down' (HC, 137, 661), a statement which he supported with evidence from the 1851 census, from which he concluded that over 46 per cent of the nation's children were neither at school nor at work. Nevertheless, in view of the fact that of well over twelve thousand schools supported by religious bodies, ten and a half thousand were run by the Church, he maintained that any solution would have to be along denominational rather than secular lines. He urged the Secularists seriously to face up to the question of whether they had the power to enforce their system when the greater proportion of schools were in the hands of the Anglicans.

His question certainly seems to have been taken seriously, for immediately members of both Manchester organizations, led by Cobden and Canon Richson in consultation with Pakington, began serious discussions resulting, in 1857, in the formation of a new pressure group called the General Committee on Education. The Manchester and Salford Committee meanwhile disbanded in 1855, and the NPSA followed its example in 1862. The bill of this new body, proposing a locally-administered rate for secular instruction in denominational schools without disturbing their management, was introduced into the Commons on 18 February 1857. Ironically, it ran out of time as a result of Cobden's motion of censure on Palmerston's aggressive policy towards China.

In the new short-lived Tory government, Pakington was First Lord of the Admiralty, but he did not reintroduce the measure. Instead, in 1858 he moved an address proposing the appointment of a Royal Commission 'to consider and report what measures, if any, are required for the extension of sound and cheap elementary instruction to all classes of the people'. Hence the Newcastle Commission was summoned, the deliberations of which will be examined in a later chapter.

Education and mid-nineteenth-century politics

So far as Manchester is concerned, 1857 marks not only the end of its initiatives in secular education, but also the end of its period of Radical leadership. The foundation of the General Committee on Education signified that the Manchester reformers had, for the time being, abandoned the secular cause as hopeless, and that future solutions to the education problem in Manchester would be sought along denominational rather than secular lines, whilst the devastating defeat of Cobden, Bright, Milner, Gibson and Fox in the general election of 1857 marked the end of the period of influence of the League faction in South Lancashire. The nature of Manchester Liberalism becomes much more moderate after that date and so, in consequence, do its policies on social reform.

Immediately after his defeat in 1857, John Bright was elected Liberal MP for Birmingham. Significantly, it was that town which, under the leadership of Joseph Chamberlain, assumed Manchester's mantle of Radical leadership and took up the struggle for national secular education at the point where the NPSA had left it. As will be seen, the

Birmingham middle-class Radicals enjoyed the support of an articulate Labour aristocracy represented by the Amalgamated Societies. Already in the 1850s the germ of these developments can be detected in the activities of William Newton, a founder of the Amalgamated Society of Engineers, the first of the Amalgamated Societies, which was founded in 1850. Newton, in his journal *The Englishman*, attacked the sectarian interference which prevented educational advance and kept the people 'in that state of ignorance which is made the ground of their exclusion from political power' (Simon, 1960, p. 343). The voluntary system, he declared, was 'one of the greatest shams of the age', giving to wealthy bigots 'the privilege of confining the system of education to one of an illiberal and intolerant nature' (ibid.). Ideas such as these combined with the effect of G. J. Holyoake's secularist movement, which attracted thousands of skilled labourers in the 1860s, were to ensure the support of organized labour for the secular education programme of the National Education League, Birmingham's successor to the NPSA.

Had the Manchester reformers failed? In terms of their legislative objectives they had failed abysmally, but in the political climate of the 1850s this was virtually inevitable. They were attempting to arouse enthusiasm for reform in a period of complacency, as H. J. Hanham has written:

> For twenty years after the end of the 'hungry forties' men were too busy taking advantage of the good times which had come to them, and sampling the pleasures of their new-found power abroad, to care much for their abstract rights. There was, as a consequence, a general desire among all but convinced reformers to shelve questions of reform until Lord Palmerston should retire (Hanham, 1959, p. xiii).

A further complication arose from the shifting and unpredictable nature of party affiliations into Parliament. The Tories had been split asunder by Peel's action over the Corn Laws, and the Whigs remained divided after their defeat in 1841. Consequently, the 1850s were characterized by a succession of weak governments which showed no desire to grapple with educational reform in a situation in which most people appreciated the need for extension of elementary education, but preferred the voluntary system to the alternative of surrendering their vested interests to the state. The Secularists were particularly troubled by the current political fragmentation, as Cobden ruefully explained in 1854:

> In former times, if you had a movement for reform, you have had one political party, at all events, pretty generally unanimous with you; but what have we to counter in this educational movement? We have had cross-fires from every side against us; on one side the

Church, on the other side a portion of dissenters ably led by Mr Baines (NPSA Report, 17 January 1854).

It was ironic that the very factor which had united Radical Dissent since 1843, opposition to state intervention in education, was inimical to the programme of the secular Radicals (Perkin, 1969, p. 352).

Under these circumstances, all that the Manchester reformers could hope to do was to educate public opinion in the intricacies and alternatives within the scope of educational reform. As Sir John Pakington admitted with reference to the education bills that he sponsored: 'I merely brought them forward as embodying my own views, but I was always conscious of the difficulties of the question, and never supposed that hon. members would pass those Bills into a Law' (HC, 148, 1194).

Yet this was only a short-term failure, because 'in the Manchester Debate all possibilities had been discussed and advocated' (Read, 1964, p. 169), and the consensus reached within the General Committee on Education was to make an invaluable contribution to the achievement of Forster's measure of 1870.

Chapter three

The education of a nation

There may have been no great legislative leap forward in elementary education during the 1850s, but this did not insulate educational institutions from the spate of Benthamite reform which had already rationalized the electoral system, the Poor Law, public health and the fiscal system. In fact, between 1850 and 1868 four Royal Commissions made recommendations which initiated the modernization of the older universities, promoted the adaptation of the public and endowed grammar schools to contemporary needs, and brought the rapidly expanding elementary schools within closer control of the central authority. It was, moreover, highly appropriate that the Act which opened up Oxford University to reform in 1854 should be passed in the same year that the principle of competitive examination was introduced for recruitment into the home civil service in the aftermath of the Northcote-Trevelyan report, for already the older universities, and Balliol College in particular, had begun to provide the pool of ability from which the expanding government service was to obtain its new professional administrators. As early as 1832, Sir Henry Taylor, clerk to the colonial office, remarking on the growing complexity of government and the need to focus 'more knowledge both general and particular' on public affairs, had argued for the substitution of selection by merit in place of the older practice of granting clerkships to 'the sons of people of rank and influence brought up in idleness'. Unfortunately, as he lamented with reference to the situation in the 1830s, 'in our state of transition influence has been left behind and efficiency we have not yet reached' (Perkin, 1969, p. 336).

The educational reforms of the 1850s and 1860s were to go a long way toward providing the efficiency that Taylor demanded. Of equal importance, however, is their social significance. Since the early part of the century middle-class Radicals had been demanding access to and reform of hitherto closed educational corporations, and the legislation which followed the Royal Commissions on the universities of Oxford and Cambridge, the Public Schools and the Endowed Grammar Schools can be interpreted as a response to these demands. Curiously enough, however, although the reforms were Benthamite in origin, Bentham's utilitarian Chrestomathic scheme did not become the educational model for the rising middle classes. Instead, having exposed the deficiencies of the existing educational institutions and acquiesced in the attempts to organize them in accordance with the Victorian social hierarchy, the middle classes, mollified by their growing power and relatively easy access to wealth, were content to share their benefits with the aristocracy and gentry without radically changing their function or curricula.

Only the working classes at the base of society were to receive a strictly utilitarian education, but that was to be expected for, despite their considerable financial contribution to education, much of what they received was provided at the hands of their more fortunate social superiors, whose conception of working-class educational needs, as the *Newcastle Report* was to reveal, was strictly limited.

The reform of the older universities

The universities of Oxford and Cambridge were the first of the educational institutions to be investigated. Held in a clerical stranglehold which severely limited their functions, their narrow range of studies dominated by classics at Oxford and mathematics at Cambridge, coupled with the fact that none but Anglicans were permitted to graduate, made them ready targets for the criticisms of middle-class Radicals. Fortunately all the pressure was not from outside, for each university had its reforming party, represented by people such as Goldwin Smith and Benjamin Jowett at Oxford, and Adam Sedgwick the geologist at Cambridge. Desirous, however, as these men were to open the universities to men of ability, their reforming efforts were completely frustrated by the power of the individual colleges and the conservative forces within them. The Tractarians at Oxford were the most formidable obstacle. Aiming essentially to reconcile Anglicanism with Roman Catholicism, they effectively blocked any reforms which might lessen the clerical hold upon the university. The problem was only solved when the movement was discredited, in 1845, by J. H. Newman's conversion to Catholicism, the result of which, in the words of Mark Pattison, was to open up the universities to 'a flood of reform . . . which did not spend itself 'till it had produced two government commissions, until we ourselves had enlarged and remodelled our institutions'. There was much lost ground to be made up, for, as Pattison went on to indicate, 'the great discoveries of the last century were not even known by report to any of us. Science was placed under a ban by the theologians who instinctively felt that it was fatal to their speculations' (Pattison, 1885, 1969 edn, pp. 236—8).

Fortunately, external agitation came to the aid of the reformers, notably in the pages of the *Edinburgh Review*, where Sir William Hamilton, attacking the universities for ineffective teaching, misuse of endowments, and their requirement of subscriptions to the Thirty-nine Articles, concluded: 'It is from the State only, and the Crown in particular, that we can reasonably hope for an academical reformation worthy of the name' (*Edinburgh Review*, December 1831, p. 499). Finally, after continuous pressure throughout the 1830s and 1840s, the motion of James Heywood, MP for North Lancashire, to appoint a Royal Commission to enquire into the working of the two universities was accepted by the government and the Royal Commission was issued in August 1850. This was highly appropriate, for Heywood, a Unitarian banker, was himself a former Cambridge student who had been prevented from taking his degree by the religious test.

The composition of the two Royal Commissions, which included Oxford and Cambridge men who desired reform, left no doubt as to the intentions of the government, and despite great opposition from the universities, particularly Oxford, the commissioners contrived to amass a sufficient body of evidence on which to base their recommendations.

In general they found that the number of students was small because the education offered was irrelevant to all who did not wish to enter the Church. The lack of incentive to work, which according to Mark Pattison's evidence led to degeneration and seduction by 'the three great temptations of the place . . . fornication, wine and betting' (Simon, 1960, p. 294), and the religious test, limited the range of potential students. As for the curriculum, only a few students were affected by the honours-degree examination, the majority remaining largely unoccupied. Professional training in law and medicine had virtually ceased, while even training for the clergy was found to be deficient. In addition, the whole collegiate structure was declared to be defective.

With great significance for the future, the commissioners concluded that the government had the right to intervene in the universities on the grounds that they were national institutions. Accordingly the opening up of these hitherto closed corporations was initiated by the Oxford University Act of 1854 and the Cambridge University Act of 1856, as a result of which university government was democratized, the development of scientific and modern studies was made possible, college statutes were modernized and ancient privileges removed. Nonconformists, however, although now permitted to take first degrees, had to wait until 1871 before Gladstone removed their remaining disabilities, and even then the universities remained predominantly Anglican institutions. Nevertheless, the older universities could now gradually adapt to the demands of the new modern state. Of broader significance, however, as W. L. Burn indicated, was the radical theory of government action which underlay these relatively mild reforms, for 'in order to serve what we might today call the "national interest", vested rights were invaded and the practices of private societies were amended to conform with what was held to be nationally desirable' (Burn, 1964, 1968 edn, p. 149).

Public school reform

Now that the walls of privilege had been undermined, there was nothing to save further 'private societies' – for instance, the public schools – from investigation. These were defined by the Clarendon Commission, which investigated them between 1861 and 1864, as Eton, Winchester, Westminster, St Paul's, Merchant Taylors', Charterhouse, Harrow, Shrewsbury and Rugby. By the middle of the nineteenth century the social composition of these schools was changing. They were no longer monopolized by the aristocracy and the gentry, for the upper-middle classes, encouraged by the new Arnoldian public school image, had begun to infiltrate them. Yet in spite of this they left much to be desired.

From the 1820s, as with the universities, middle-class critics had found a ready target in the deplorable moral state and barbaric living conditions of these schools and their almost completely classical curricula. 'The Eton boy', stated the *Westminster Review* in 1835, was likely, before reaching university age, to have acquired 'a confirmed taste for gluttony and drunkenness, an aptitude for brutal sports, and a passion for female society of the most degrading kind' (Simon, op. cit., pp. 101–2). Moreover, in an era when a good education for the ruling class was defined in terms of a training for the mind, there was little incentive to introduce its sons to the utilitarian sciences. It was assumed that the classics could provide 'all the principle and mental discipline required to train the statesman, the divine and the gentleman' (ibid., p. 300). Even Thomas Arnold, interested in science, a friend of scientists, and a notorious believer in the ultimate beneficence of industrialization, could inform the members of the Rugby Mechanics' Institute:

> Physical science alone can never make a man educated, even the formal sciences (grammar, arithmetic, logic, geometry), valuable as they are with respect to the discipline of the reasoning powers, cannot instruct the judgement; it is only moral and religious knowledge which can accomplish this (Bamford, 1967, p. 92).

Education to Arnold was a matter for personal development, and

31

therefore unrelated to anything so utilitarian as national survival.

Such complacency could not last, however, in the changing social and economic environment of the nineteenth century. Fears began to grow that ignorance of science and technology among the land-holding aristocracy and gentry constituted a threat to the maintenance of their social supremacy. For, as Baden Powell, Professor of Geometry at Oxford, had warned as early as 1832: 'Scientific knowledge is rapidly spreading among all classes except the Higher, and the consequence must be that class will not long remain the Higher' (ibid., p. 106). Meanwhile, the establishment of the successful proprietary boarding schools, serving the professional and industrial classes, such as Cheltenham, Marlborough, and Rossall, which prepared pupils for careers in commerce, the army, the civil service, colonial administration and the Church, added to the general anxiety. As the Earl of Clarendon stated, the fear grew that the prevailing inefficiency of established public schools would place 'the upper classes in a state of inferiority to the middle and lower' (Mack, 1941, p. 27).

Matters were finally brought to a head in 1861 when, in the wake of M. J. Higgins's bitter criticisms of Eton in the *Cornhill Magazine* and Sir J. T. Coleridge's Tiverton lecture on the same theme, an article in the *Edinburgh Review* actually accused the teachers of the upper classes of embezzlement, in that 'revenues willed by an English king for the promotion of education amongst the upper and middle classes of this country' had been diverted 'into the pockets of a small number of individuals' who were not entitled to them (*Edinburgh Review*, April 1861, p. 45), a situation which Lord Brougham had revealed forty years earlier.

The author's demand for a Royal Commission to investigate this state of affairs bore fruit three months later upon the setting up of the Public Schools Commission 'to inquire into the Revenues and management of certain Colleges and Schools and the studies pursued and instruction given therein'. Its members, presided over by Lord Clarendon, revealed a catalogue of abuses. For example, in corroboration of the allegations of corruption the evidence revealed that during the previous twenty years, the Provost and the Fellows of Eton had successfully pocketed a sum of £127,700 which should have been spent on the college. Of the nine schools, in fact, only Rugby escaped unblemished. As for their curriculum, again with the exception of Rugby, not only was science virtually non-existent but even the teaching of classics, the schools' staple commodity, was inefficient (*Clarendon Report*, ii, p. 49). There was also much time wasting and a severe lack of intellectual progress (ibid., i, p. 26).

The commissioners responded by recommending a radical transformation of governing bodies to enable the schools to meet contemporary needs in public and professional life. Classics, however, was to be retained as a social distancing agent, the hallmark of an upper-class education. At the same time the curriculum was to be broadened by the inclusion of mathematics, modern languages, history, geography, English composition, and natural science, a subject currently taught only at Rugby. Even so, classics was to occupy half the curriculum and science a mere eighth.

Nevertheless, the schools did not escape the hand of Bentham, for in order to infuse a greater degree of purpose into their teaching the commissioners recommended more academic competition, the award of prizes for merit, examinations and the daily marking of work; practices adopted at Shrewsbury by Samuel Butler at the beginning of the century. Finally, in order to ensure the social exclusiveness of the schools, the practice of excluding poor scholars and local pupils in favour of fee payers and open scholars was recommended for general adoption.

These recommendations were finally sanctioned by the Public Schools Act of 1868. They were by no means radical, but merely sought to rehabilitate the schools while at the same time preserving their social exclusiveness. Not only did they succeed in doing this but, by creating 'a consensus of upper-class opinion, a compromise between the educational ideas dominant among the Victorian middle class and the aristocracy' (Mack, op cit., pp. 29–30), they also played a crucial role in the formation of the late Victorian social structure.

The reform of middle-class education

Of much greater complexity than the task of reforming the public schools was the problem of devising some efficient form of education for the middle classes, 'those large classes of English society which are comprised between the humblest and the very highest'. It was made all the harder by the diverse nature of their educational needs, which were seen as a quasi-public school education for the professional class at the upper end and the kind provided in the more efficient private schools for tradesmen and artisans at the lower.

The problem was intensified by the growing realization by the middle classes of their own political importance, clearly expressed in 1824 in the *Westminster Review* by one of their spokesmen:

> It is the strength of the community. It contains beyond all comparison the greatest proportion of the intelligence, industry and the wealth of the state. In it are the heads that invent and the hands that execute . . . ; the men, in fact, who think for the rest of the world, and who really do the business of this world, are the men of this class (*Westminster Review*, 1824, pp. 68–9).

For these reasons, concluded the article, and considering that both the working and upper classes were under its control, 'the proper education of this portion of the people is therefore of the greatest possible importance to the well-being of the state' (ibid.).

The aristocracy and the gentry were no less conscious of the increasing influence of this section of the community. They clearly saw the need to persuade the middle classes that their interests lay with them, and not with the working classes. As a Scottish memorandum on political reform to Lord John Russell stated in 1830, 'It is of the utmost importance to associate the middle with the higher orders of society in the love and support of the institutions and the government of the country' (Gash, 1953, p. 15).

Unfortunately, the educational machinery for promoting this desired harmony of class interests was sadly defective. An efficient system of schools would at least have held out the hope to the middle classes of maintaining their social status, but unfortunately the vast majority of endowed grammar schools which might have been expected to serve this purpose were either grossly inefficient, unevenly distributed, or both. Consequently the first half of the nineteenth century witnessed a number of attempts to remedy the situation.

Bentham's Chrestomathic utilitarian ideal middle-class school never achieved any degree of permanence (Simon, op. cit., p. 109). Nevertheless the more realistic curriculum which he advocated, and which the lower middle classes demanded, was partially supplied by a proliferation of proprietary and private schools, alongside the grammar schools. Meanwhile, in the late 1830s the National Society, motivated by the fears of state intervention and guided by Lord Ashley, Lord Sandon and W. E. Gladstone, sponsored a short-lived attempt to establish middle-class schools for 'the higher branches of instruction' in both rural and urban areas (Roach, 1971, p. 45). Probably the most notable experiments, however, were those carried out by the High Anglican clergyman Nathaniel Woodard and J. L. Brereton, vicar of West Buckland in North Devon, for both anticipated the proposals later made by the Taunton Commissioners, in that their schemes were hierarchical in conception. Woodard, for example, in his pamphlet *A Plea for the Middle Classes* (1848), envisaged schools for gentlemen of limited means in the first grade, tradesmen and farmers in the second, and small tradesmen and hucksters in the third.

In spite of these efforts, however, the problem remained unsolved, and it became clear once again that if, as Thomas Arnold had urged in 1832, the 'middling classes' were to be provided with 'something analogous to the advantages offered to the rich classes by our great public schools and universities' (ibid., p. 40), government intervention was imperative. Consequently in 1864, in response to a memorial presented by the National Association for the Promotion of Social

Science, representing the culmination of half a century of agitation, Lord Palmerston set up the Schools Enquiry Commission under the chairmanship of Lord Taunton, which proceeded to carry out the most thorough and uncompromising of all the educational enquiries.

Classics or charity?

The Commissioners had certain precedents before them as guides to their deliberations. They noted that a large proportion of endowed grammar schools had declined to the level of inefficient elementary schools and, therefore, were failing to attract the middle classes. Moreover, they concluded, their failure, contrary to the opinion of J. L. Brereton, Frederick Temple, Robert Lowe, Herbert Spencer, and other commentators, was not due to their dogged adherence to the classics, many of them having abandoned teaching them. Paradoxically, the evidence appeared to show that the converse was nearer the truth. The well-attended schools which did exist, for example at Manchester, Norwich, St Peter's York, and Leeds, were primarily teaching the classics and, furthermore, these were the schools which had already established the right to admit fee-payers prior to the setting up of the Commission (Balls, 1967, p. 209).

The explanation lies in the growing demand from the professional middle classes for a first-class education, promising social mobility by means of access to Oxford and Cambridge and the newly expanding career opportunities in the army and the civil and colonial services, at a price cheaper than anything available at a public school. Consequently, the Commissioners determined to rehabilitate the grammar schools by enabling them to open themselves up to this wider-spread, moderately-affluent, fee-paying clientele.

In pursuing their objective, however, they were inevitably acting against the interests of the lower middle-class tradesmen and artisans, many of whose sons occupied the free places provided by the founders of grammar schools for the benefit of poor children of the locality, in preference to the socially inferior, but sometimes more efficient, state-supported elementary schools. Even where grammar schools were not available they often preferred to use private schools of dubious quality rather than allow their children to mix with the elementary-school clientele (ibid.), although there were some exceptions to this rule, as James Bryce noted in Manchester (Simon, op. cit., p. 322). It was generally believed, however, that they got a bad bargain, as Sir John Pakington indicated in 1857: 'It is the respectable tradesmen, the small farmer, the clerk, and the men of that description who know not where to get education for their children, and who pay very dearly for a bad article' (*The Times*, 20 June 1864). The Taunton Commissioners, therefore, wishing to promote the social aspirations of this lowest stratum of the middle classes, recognized that the greatest need was to provide them with third-rate, non-classical schools which, nevertheless, would be secondary rather than elementary in status.

The Taunton Commission's findings

The findings of the assistant Commissioners largely confirmed the previous reports of the grammar schools' deplorable condition. Of some 782 endowed schools, only 209 could be considered as genuine classical schools, while of the others 340 taught neither classics nor any other subject with efficiency. The schools were, in general, ill-housed and ill-equipped, as indicated by James Bryce (*Taunton Report*, ix, pp. 490–1) in Lancashire, and J. G. Fitch (ibid., p. 177) in Yorkshire. In contrast, the middle-class proprietary schools which had begun to appear in the larger towns were generally found to be efficient (ibid., i, p. 314), but the private schools, with few exceptions, were considered to be very bad indeed.

Bryce's observations in Manchester and Liverpool are particularly fascinating, illustrating how particular schools were patronized by distinct social groups and how certain schools excluded pupils on social grounds; a process illustrated at Liverpool College, which was a middle class in microcosm, its three constituent schools corresponding 'to the three divisions of society', the pupils being kept 'quite apart from one another except at the daily prayers at opening the school' (ibid., p. 317).

The Commissioners were particularly interested in the evidence provided by the Rev. James Fraser and Matthew Arnold; the former having been to New England and the latter to France, Germany, Switzerland and Italy. Fraser considered the New England high schools to be inferior to the best schools in England, but he was impressed both by the lower-grade schools and by the teachers, who were lively, interesting, and commanded good discipline (ibid., p. 321). It was nevertheless the Prussian system, as described by Arnold, which most impressed the Commissioners, and which they considered to be superior to anything that either the Americans or the French could offer. Moreover, unlike the radicals of the National Public School Association, they were favourably disposed to the Prussian educational bureaucracy. Equally significant, however, in view of the final report, was their admiration for the way in which the schools met 'every possible need of every class' by means of three grades. The Gymnasien and the first grade of the Realschulen provided a nine-year course to the age of eighteen, the second grade Realschulen a seven-year course, and the third grade, or Burgerschulen, a still shorter course; the length of course determining the social class of the clientele.

The Commissioners, nevertheless, considered that it would be both 'useless and impracticable' to try to transplant an entire foreign system into England, but saw no reason why they should not do something of a corresponding character. Accordingly, their proposals would have grafted English secondary education onto a carefully articulated hierarchical administrative framework of central and local control, had not middle-class opposition to state intervention prevented most of them from being implemented.

Envisaging a national system of secondary education with the existing endowed schools as the core, the Commissioners defined three grades of schools according to the social class of their clientele. The first grade, including the public schools, proprietary schools like Clifton and Haileybury, and grammar schools with a national intake of pupils such as Uppingham and Oundle, would provide a mainly classical education to the age of eighteen for the children of the aristocracy and gentry, the higher professional classes and wealthy industrialists. Second-grade schools would serve the smaller professional and businessmen's children, providing an education up to sixteen in Latin, English Literature, political economy, mathematics and science, while schools of the third grade would serve the lower-middle and upper-working classes up to the age of fourteen with a curriculum comprising the elements of Latin or a foreign language, English history, elementary mathematics, geography and science. The social exclusiveness and 'efficiency' of the schools, meanwhile, was to be ensured by the abolition of 'indiscriminate gratuitous instruction', the only means of free entry being by means of exhibitions to be competed for by all comers; a provision which was virtually guaranteed to benefit the middle classes.

Of a much more radical nature than the proposed school reforms, however, was the envisaged administrative structure in which W. L. Burn discerned 'that search for the overriding authority, that passion for supra-individual efficiency, which both imperial proconsuls and members of the Fabian Society were before long to display' (Burn, op. cit., p. 201). A central authority presided over by a Minister of Education was to be responsible for drawing up proposals for school reorganization, below which provincial authorities in the form of District Commissioners or, alternatively, county and town boards, would have control of the schools, through boards of governors. A Council of Examinations was to be constituted to devise rules for conducting examinations and vetting the qualifications of teachers, all of whom ultimately would be required to possess a teaching certificate. Other recommendations that all parishes should be able to rate themselves for the provision of third-grade schools anticipated the 1902 Act and advertised further the commissioners' anxiety on behalf of the lower-middle class. Finally, in addition to making vitally important recommendations for reorganizing the management of schools, the Commissioners, pressed by that great champion of women's education, Emily Davies, interpreted their terms of reference broadly enough to enable them to urge that, where-ever possible, endowment funds should be allocated for the provision of girls' secondary schools.

The implementation of the report

These radical-collectivist proposals, however, turned out to be prema-ture, for the Gladstone government, opposed on the one hand by the Church over its attempts to lower the grade of some schools, and on the other by the lower-middle class arguing in the name of the poor against the removal of their rights to free entry, contented itself with establish-ing an Endowed Schools Commission by means of the Endowed Schools Act of 1869. Nevertheless, by 1874, when it was disbanded by the Conservatives and its function transferred to the Charity Commis-sion for being too sanguine in its work, this body had succeeded in drawing up 317 schemes of reform, 97 of which had been before Parlia-ment, and many more were in preparation. Moreover, its efforts on behalf of girls' schools were so energetic that it has been credited with inaugurating 'a new era in girls' education' (Archer, 1921, p. 169), to the extent that by 1898 there were over eighty endowed girls' schools (ibid., p. 247), whereas previously there had been virtually none.

Of even greater significance was the change wrought by the new schemes in the management of schools. Previously the headmaster of an endowed school had on appointment been presented with its freehold, which meant that it was almost impossible to dismiss him no matter how gross his inefficiency. Such practices, however, were not in accord-ance with the growing interventionist ethos of the mid-nineteenth cen-tury. 'No man,' reported the Taunton Commission, 'in founding a per-manent school . . . can have intended his schools to be inefficient; and if he had, the State would not be justified in permitting it to be perma-nent' (*Taunton Report*, i, p. 224). Consequently, the new schemes deprived the headmaster of his freehold, vested the power of his appointment and dismissal with the school governors, and in turn, as an incentive to efficiency, gave him the power to appoint and dismiss his assistant masters. Thus the relationship between these three ele-ments of school management was completely transformed.

Ironically it is difficult to avoid the conclusion that the realloca-tion of endowments was done at the expense of the very class that the Commissioners had wanted to provide for: the skilled artisans, clerks and small tradesmen, in order to subsidize the education of the more affluent groups of the same social class, who in any case could afford to pay fees. Certainly the objections to reorganization described in the

Report of the Select Committee on Endowed Schools Act, 1869, 1887 (Simon, op. cit., p. 331) at Scarning in Norfolk, Kendal and Sutton Coldfield support this view. Moreover, as the Bryce Commission reported, third-grade schools were never established in sufficient numbers to cater for their intended clientele who eventually were obliged to patronize the higher-grade elementary schools established by the larger school boards. The reforms thereby reinforced 'what has remained the real social barrier in England, not, essentially, between rich and poor, but between the professional and non-professional classes' (Balls, 1968, p. 227). Nevertheless, these reservations notwithstanding, the foundations of an articulated, albeit highly stratified, system of secondary education had been laid.

The Newcastle Commission

The Newcastle Commission's investigation of elementary education began in 1858, four years after the investigation of the older universities and before the Clarendon and Taunton Commissions, but its concern with the education of the classes at the base of the social hierarchy provides an appropriate reason to consider it last of all. As already noted in the first two chapters, any disquiet occasioned by the state of middle-class education was mild compared with the deep-seated anxiety aroused by the problem of educating the nation's poor. Yet the report of the Commission summoned in response to Sir John Pakington's motion in 1858 was in some respects the least radical of all.

In view of the uncertainty of the Palmerston ministry, however, and the shifting nature of Parliamentary alignments already referred to in the previous chapter, the unadventurous nature of the Commission's proposals is hardly surprising. Moreover, the constraints on government with regard to elementary education were much greater than those associated with secondary and university education, involving, as they did, financial and religious considerations with regard to the distribution of the exchequer grant and the constitutional problem of the delicate relationship between Parliament and Committee of Council. The latter difficulty arose out of the quasi-legislative machinery by which, in the absence of statutory legislation, the Education Department carried on its business; namely through Committee of Council Minutes. To many MPs such methods appeared to enable the Education Department to expand its operations, and proportionally its expenditure, under a cloud of obscurity, giving rise to questions of where responsibility for elementary education actually lay.

The appointment in 1856 of a Vice-President of the Council sitting in the Commons was an attempt to allay such anxieties, but this achieved no solution at all because the new minister was obliged to share responsibility for education with the Lord President and the nebulous Committee of Council. A decade later, in *Schools and Universities on the Continent*, Matthew Arnold was still lamenting 'that at present, with our Lord President, Vice-President and Committee of Council on Education, we entirely fail to get, for primary instruction, this distinct centre of responsibility' (Arnold, 1868, p. 196).

In these circumstances the Palmerston ministry was hardly likely to cause itself more trouble than necessary, having no desire to be defeated over the complex matter of elementary education. The choice of membership of the Royal Commission was, therefore, crucially important as Ralph Lingen, Kay-Shuttleworth's successor as Secretary to the Committee of Council on Education, made clear in a letter to the Lord President, Lord Granville: 'I should be very sorry to see any very pronounced advocates of the present system among the commissioners. Such men are deaf to everything but the cry for larger grants' (Williams, 1973, p. 63). There was obviously no room for Kay-Shuttleworth and others of a zealous disposition towards education. Even Pakington was viewed with disfavour as Lord Granville made clear to Cowper, the Vice-President of the Committee of Council: 'Whatever you do, don't put Pakington on it . . . it would be injurious to the cause and inconvenient to the government' (ibid., p. 64). Accordingly, no Members of Parliament were appointed to the seven-man commission, of which only Nassau Senior favoured any further extension of state intervention (Senior, 1861, p. 34).

The Commission's findings

In spite of these limitations, the Newcastle Commission, whose task it was to enquire into the *State of Popular Education in England*, as the report was entitled, and more important, to suggest how 'sound and cheap elementary instruction' could be extended to the whole population, carried out the most thorough examination of elementary education to date.

Assistant Commissioners were sent to ten sample areas, while in order to acquire comparative evidence Mark Pattison was despatched to Germany and Matthew Arnold to France, Switzerland and Holland. In addition the provision made for paupers, criminals and vagrants, the military and naval schools, and charitable endowments was also investigated.

The Report confirmed that although since the establishment of the Committee of Council in 1839 the role of the state had been limited to assisting voluntary effort, the government grant had, nevertheless, reached the sum of £798,000 by 1860. Since 1850 the number of day schools had grown from 46,042 to 58,975 and the number of pupils from 2,144,378 to 2,535,462, representing 1 in 7·7 of the population; a significant improvement on the ratio of 1 in 8 reported by the census of 1851 (*Newcastle Report,* i, p. 87).

Of these children, however, it was estimated that only 920,000 were in grant-aided schools, leaving a million and a quarter who were not. Bringing this latter group within the orbit of state-assistance would, therefore, raise a difficult financial problem for which a solution would have to be devised if the Commission were to carry out its brief.

Concluding from the evidence that 'almost all the children in the country capable of going to school receive some instruction', the Commissioners had nevertheless to admit that they left early, attended irregularly, and tended to move from school to school, 17·4 per cent attending for less than fifty days a year. Just under two-thirds, however, attended for twenty weeks a year or more, as a result of which it was assumed that they would be able to learn to read and write, and to perform 'such arithmetical operations as occur in the ordinary business of life!' (ibid., p. 174). In fact, despite their complaint about the brevity of school life, the Commissioners treated the matter with a certain complacent resignation, quoting with approval James Fraser's view of the education of the working-class child: 'We must make up our minds to see the last of him, as far as the day school is concerned, at 10 or 11' (ibid., p. 243). After all, they argued, 'the peremptory demands of the labour market' required that this should be the rule; moreover, 'if the wages of the child's labour are necessary, either to keep the parents from the poor rates, or to relieve the pressure of severe and bitter poverty, it is far better that it should go to work at the earliest age at which it can bear the physical exertion than that it should remain at school' (ibid., p. 188).

Compulsory education, therefore, in spite of the desire expressed for it by the miners of Durham and Bristol, was not recommended, the Commissioners having interpreted Matthew Arnold's report to mean that good attendance in Switzerland was more a function of local prosperity than legal enforcement, and Mark Pattison's to prove that Prussian legal sanctions were superfluous, regular school attendance having been a national habit since the Reformation (ibid., p. 195). They were also influenced by the results of a questionnaire, to which the majority of respondents declared themselves against a general system of compulsory education (ibid., p. 197). It is interesting, however, to note Matthew Arnold's rejoinder to the interpretation of his evidence by those whom he described as 'the opponents of compulsory education'. A constant admirer of state-controlled, Continental systems of education, he was anxious to put the record straight:

The example of the Continent proves, and nothing which Mr Pattison or I have said disproves that in general, where popular education is most prosperous, there it is also compulsory. The compulsoriness is, in general, found to go along with prosperity, though it cannot be said to cause it, but the same high value among people for education which leads to its prospering among them, leads also in general to its being made compulsory (Arnold, op. cit., p. xvii).

Probably the factor which weighed most heavily with the Commissioners, however, was the potential effect of legal enforcement on the role of the state, with its implication for provision of free education. For, as they realized, 'that which the state compels it must also enable men to do' (*Newcastle Report*, i, p. 200), and to ask the state to interfere in people's lives to such an extent was considered to be more collectivist than public opinion would tolerate in 1861.

The Commission's recommendations

In making their recommendations the Commission recognized four weaknesses in the current system: expense, the problem of the poorer districts, defective teaching, and an over-centralized administrative structure.

Expense, in the form of the Treasury grant, which had quadrupled between 1851 and 1858, stood at £789,167 in 1861, the largest civil item of government expenditure (Hurt, 1971, p. 186). Yet if all the children of school age were to be brought into the state-supported system the Commissioners envisaged an annual rent in the region of £2,100,000 (*Newcastle Report*, i, p. 314), which was a particularly alarming prospect in view of the regularity of the amendments to reduce the education vote moved in Parliament since 1854 (Hurt, op. cit., p. 188). Moreover, the Treasury's inability either to control expenditure or to calculate how much would be expended in a particular year hardly improved matters. Furthermore, the extension of the exchequer grant to mainly rural poorer districts, it was estimated, would add another £200,000 a year to the cost. An operation on this scale, therefore, would require the levying of a local rate in order to relieve the burden on the exchequer, and would necessitate some degree of local control. Defective teaching, meanwhile, which was interpreted as the teacher's natural inclination to concentrate on the brighter children, resulting, so the Commissioners alleged, in only a quarter of them being thoroughly taught, demanded the provision of inducements to persuade schoolmasters to spend more time with their younger pupils (*Newcastle Report*, i, p. 320). Finally, the concentration of detailed administration in the central office, resulting from Kay-Shuttleworth's Minutes of 1846, necessitating the payment in 1859 of a total of £252,550. 12s 11d. on 20,000 separate money orders to individual pupil-teachers and teachers, cried out for some drastic act of decentralization if the system was to be extended.

The Commissioners accordingly proposed a simplified grant system of two types: an exchequer grant paid to schools, denominational or otherwise, based on attendance and the fulfilment of certain physical conditions, and a grant paid out of the rates, administered by County and Town Boards, allocated according to examination results in reading, writing, arithmetic, and plain needlework for girls; the total amount earnable never to exceed fifteen shillings per child.

The Revised Code

The Revised Code of 1862, which was the instrument with which the *Newcastle Report* was implemented, shelved the idea of a county rate, but adopted the other recommendations for allocating the exchequer grant. Introduced originally in July 1861 by Robert Lowe, the irascible Vice-President of the Council, this scheme, better known as 'payment by results', permitted children below the age of six to earn a grant of six shillings and six pence each on attendance alone. Children over six could earn four shillings according to their average attendance and, in addition, two shillings and eight pence for a pass in each of the three Rs, making the maximum earnable grant twelve shillings per child over six years of age. On the results of the examination, carried out by an inspector, the managers of each school would receive a block grant.

At a stroke, therefore, the Revised Code swept away the highly centralized post-1846 grant structure, substituting in its place a simplified decentralized administrative system, the pattern of which is still with us, a simple formula for assessing the block grant, financial incentives for teachers to achieve better results, and a measurable return on investment. It was, in fact, a most appropriate scheme to have been devised by 'the last of the genuine Benthamites', as A. V. Dicey described Lowe (Dicey, 1905, 1926 edn, p. 253). Yet some of his contemporaries were less than enchanted.

In his 'Letter to Earl Granville, KG on the Revised Code' of November 1861, Kay-Shuttleworth complained bitterly that the school's enslavement to the three Rs by the operation of the code would debilitate it as a civilizing agency (Kay-Shuttleworth, 1862, pp. 574–638). Meanwhile, Matthew Arnold, noting that 'Shuttleworth has just published a most important pamphlet . . . it sells like wildfire' (Connell, 1950, p. 211), decided himself to supply 'a reasonable popular statement of the case'. This turned out to be his article in *Fraser's Magazine* of March 1862, deploring the fact that the state's previous concern with 'paying for discipline, for civilization, for religious and moral training, for a superior instruction to clever and forward children' was now to be abandoned in favour of lower standards of popular education (ibid., p. 212).

Yet amid the furore of opposition, there were some favourable comments. For example, the educational periodical *Papers for the Schoolmaster* welcomed the new system as a fairer way of distributing the grant, as also did the quarterly journal *Museum* (Fletcher, 1972, p. 19). Moreover, it can be argued that in stressing the need to impart basic literacy and numeracy to all elementary-school pupils the code not only provided a much-needed efficiency measure, but also asserted that the school's primary function was the inculcation of secular knowledge rather than religious indoctrination. Furthermore, the fall in grant, foreseen by both Kay-Shuttleworth and Arnold, from the 1861 figure of £813,441 to £622,730 in 1866, was not so much the result of the code itself but of the failure of the government to raise the earnable sum above twelve shillings when it became clear that the schools were suffering financially.

Nevertheless, a scheme of this nature, implemented as it was for administrative rather than educational reasons, was bound to have its drawbacks; for example, one of its results was to ensure that as a result of the operation of the grant, the elementary-school curriculum developed as a function of financial incentive rather than pedagogical theory; a possibility that Lowe never foresaw in 1862 as he characteristically explained in a letter written to Lord George Hamilton in 1878. Describing how, from his own experience in listening to the reading of boys and girls from a national school near his home, he had come to the conclusion that 'few could really read', he went on:

> I therefore came to the conclusion that as regards reading, writing and arithmetic, which are three subjects which can be definitely tested, each child should either read or write a passage, or do some simple sum of arithmetic, and the idiots who succeeded me have piled up on the top of the three Rs a mass of class and specific subjects which they propose to test in the same way (Morris, 1961, pp. 8–9).

In spite of this rationale, however, the code's emphasis on the three Rs, vividly contrasting with current attempts to broaden the curriculum of middle-class schools, carried the overwhelming implication that the function of the elementary school was to ensure the perpetuation of 'a docile and permanent labour force' (Perkin, op. cit., p. 300).

The period 1850–69, in which the state intervened in education right across the board, as we have seen, is remarkable for the manner in which social-class divisions were not only sharpened between the various segments of the education system, but also within them. As

Professor Best has written: 'Educational systems can hardly help mirroring the ideas about social relationships of the societies that produce them', the significance of these changes being that education in mid-Victorian Britain became a great 'trump card' in the great class competition. The result was that 'the schools of Britain not only mirrored the hierarchical social structure, but were made more and more to magnify its structure in detail' (Best, 1971, 1973 edn, p. 170).

Chapter four

The development of a consensus on education

Whether the purpose of a Revised Code was to provide an inherently cheap system of elementary education or whether, as is more likely, it was instigated to ensure value for money, as measured by the attendance register and the inspector's examination, the economies sustained in the mid-1860s were short lived. By 1870 the education estimates had reached £894,561; ten years later they stood at £2,487,667, easily surpassing the £2,200,000 so dreaded by the Newcastle Commission, and clearly advertising the earning potential of the new system. Furthermore, in the long run, the examination performance of thousands of school children proved to be no more predictable or controllable than had been the manipulation of the pre-1861 grant system by school managers. Nevertheless, payment by results remained the means of grant allocation until its supersession in the 1890s.

The problem of educational destitution in the 1860s, meanwhile, not only remained serious but showed every sign of intensification. Admittedly, by decentralizing the bureaucratic machine and allaying fears of over-centralization, the new code had made the extension of elementary education both politically and administratively possible. What it manifestly could not do, however, was to provide schools in areas where voluntary effort was weak, for even under payment by results passes in the annual examination were only rewarded with grants on condition that an equivalent sum was raised from voluntary sources. Consequently the voluntary system remained powerless to provide relief in the less affluent urban centres and remote rural parishes, and soon evidence from the large industrial towns, notably Manchester and Birmingham, was to point to what now was feared to be a deteriorating urban situation. It was, in fact, information of this nature, together with reactions to political events both at home, in Europe, and in the United States, described in chapter one and below, which swept aside the complacency of the *Newcastle Report*, promoting in its place a consensus in favour of a collectivist solution to the education problem. Before this could happen however, the spectacular failure of the Education Aid Societies was needed to provide final proof of the inadequacy of voluntaryism to meet the educational demands of an industrial society.

The Education Aid Societies

In his pamphlet *The Case of the Manchester Educationists*, C. H. Hinton had referred to what he considered to be the true voluntaryist solution to the education problem (Hinton, 1852, i, pp. 103–4). Describing how between 1837 and 1852 no less than 6,285 children had been persuaded to attend Sunday Schools by the Manchester Town Mission, he went on to recommend the extension of this practice by paying the school pence of destitute children in day schools; a solution which 'would be in all respects better than meeting this part of the case with a rate' (ibid.). In fact, E. R. Le Mare, an influential Salford Anglican, aided by a few friends, was already working along these lines, raising funds to pay the school fees of poor children in Manchester and Salford.

This was the embryo out of which, in 1864, grew the Manchester and Salford Education Aid Society, after the publication in the same year of the alarming revelations of Edward Brotherton, in a series of letters in the *Manchester Guardian* under the title 'The Present State of Popular Education in Manchester' (Maltby, 1918, p. 95). Brotherton, a former silk manufacturer who had retired early in order to devote himself to philanthropic activity, was convinced that the educational condition of the working classes was deteriorating, and that the problem, moreover, was mainly financial, in that children were prevented from attending school by the need to pay fees.

Accordingly, the new society, an amalgam of the former NPSA and the Manchester and Salford Committee on Education, quickly set about promoting the education of the poor 'upon such principles as may unite members of all denominations in a common effort' (ibid., p. 96). Aiming initially to enable poor children to attend school either by paying all or part of their fees, the society later hoped to establish free schools on the assumption that free education would cause the schools to be inundated with working-class children.

The outcome, however, was very wide of the mark, as J. A. Bremner informed the Manchester Congress of the National Association for the Promotion of Social Science in 1866:

In place of finding an eager demand for grants beyond the means of supply, our aid was unappreciated by many of that very class whom it was most intended to benefit. . . . In round numbers, we can only

47

succeed in sending to school about 50 per cent whose circumstances entitle them to our aid (Bremner, 1867, p. 310).

More alarming still, from their investigation of over seven thousand families in 1865, the society had been obliged to conclude that of every hundred children over the age of three not at work forty were at school but sixty did nothing at all. In the 1860s, therefore, just as in the previous decade, it was this particular group of unschooled and unemployed children who caused the greatest alarm and cast widespread doubt on the efficacy of the voluntary system. As Bremner pointed out: 'This is convincing proof that the alarm felt concerning the want of education among the manual-labour class is but too well grounded, and that former estimates are even below the truth' (ibid., p. 311). The 'thunderclap from Manchester', as H. A. Bruce later called it, reverberated elsewhere, and similar societies founded in Liverpool, Nottingham and Birmingham reported equally alarming situations, the Birmingham Education Society, for example, concluding that 'voluntary means, however generous and earnest, and however carefully organized, were powerless to combat effectually against the mass of ignorance' (Adams, 1882, pp. 193–4).

As will be seen, it was evidence of this kind, particularly from the growing industrial towns, which produced the atmosphere of crisis in which the Elementary Education Act was formulated. The urban problem, however, although very serious, was only one of a number of factors contributing to the achievement of legislation only nine years after a Royal Commission had denied its necessity.

The Liberals and the labour movement

No matter how pressing the need for a strong initiative on state education might appear in the 1860s, a major precondition for legislation was the formation of a political party with the strength and organization to undertake a programme of reform. In the event, the 'age of crisis', as it has been described (Appleman, 1959), beginning in 1859, witnessed world-wide changes, symbolic of a new era in political affairs, one repercussion of which, in England, was the passing of the Second Reform Act of 1867. Clearly, the enfranchisement by this Act of the artisan class held immense political significance for the future, but of equal importance was the manner of its passing, not only promoting the alliance between the Liberals and the Labour aristocracy, but also providing in the Liberal Party an instrument powerful enough to carry out a programme of collectivist reform.

Two crucially important agents of this process were the American Civil War and Garibaldi's visit. The Civil War enabled the labour movement, through its support for the democratic North, to present an image of sober responsibility which profoundly impressed Gladstone, helping him towards his espousal of the cause of Parliamentary Reform and his election for South Lancashire in 1865, where, 'unmuzzled', he emerged, in the words of the *Newcastle Daily Chronicle*, as the new leader of a 'Great Party of the People' (Briggs, 1959, p. 493). Garibaldi's visit in 1864, meanwhile, not only revived enthusiasm for reform, but also provided the stimulus for the foundation of the National Reform League, the indispensible crucible for the fusion of the Lib-Lab alliance upon which the new Liberal Party was based.

Both events, therefore, contributed significantly to the developments which, with the aid of Palmerston's death in 1865, the economic recession of 1866, followed by the Hyde Park riots of 23 July, presented Disraeli with the obligation to enfranchise the 'respectable' section of the working class in 1868. It was, however, the following year which saw the effective beginning of the Lib-Lab alliance, when the Liberals and the Reform League fought the 1868 election in co-operation with each other. Thus the party at the head of which Gladstone swept into power was the embodiment of the convergence of Parliamentary and popular Liberalism; a party which by the very nature of its victory was committed to social reform.

The educational implications of the Second Reform Act

The Second Reform Act inevitably set off a reaction on its own account in favour of a more efficient system of national education, the most celebrated example of which was that of Robert Lowe in his speech to the Commons on 15 July 1867. There can be few clearer statements of the Victorian perception of the interdependence of education and the franchise. Lowe urged that it was imperative to compel the nation's future political masters to learn 'their letters', for, he argued, 'from the moment that you can touch the masses with power, their education becomes an absolute necessity'. It followed, therefore, that the existing forms of educational provision would have to give way to a national system (HC, 88, 1548—9).

It must be emphasized, however, that the significance of Lowe's reaction has probably been exaggerated, for there was nothing new in the juxtaposition of education and the extension of the franchise, both middle-class and working-class reformers having consistently associated them since the early years of the century. In 1820, for example, in his article on 'Government' in the *Supplement to the Encyclopaedia Britannica*, James Mill argued on Benthamite lines for an extension of the suffrage, but only after the people had been taught where their true interests lay; an argument used in Parliament by A. J. Roebuck on introducing his resolutions in support of a national system of education in 1833. Hence education was the essential ingredient of an extended suffrage. With the same problem in mind Kay-Shuttleworth, writing in 1832, had urged the early teaching of the 'ascertained truths of political science . . . to the labouring classes' and the dissemination among them of *'correct* political information' (Kay-Shuttleworth, 1862, pp. 63–4). Meanwhile, the Chartists had been grappling with the all-important question of which should come first, schools or the vote. For William Lovett and the 'education mongers' the provision of education was the essential step towards the amelioration of the people. The *Northern Star*, on the other hand, voicing the opinion of the more militant O'Connor faction, had a different order of priorities: 'Education', it thundered in 1846, 'will follow the suffrage as day succeeds night' (Simon, 1960, p. 271); and so it did within three years.

Clearly one of the reasons why it did can be attributed to the change in attitude to education wrought by the enfranchisement of the artisan class in the minds of a number of individuals, but only in so far as it caused them to fall in behind those who had long argued for a national system. Nevertheless, as Lowe was the most extreme and articulate representative of this group, it is worth examining his personal reaction. Although well aware of the deficiencies in educational provision, he had always maintained before the Act was passed that any fundamental change would be far too difficult to make, hence his attempt to make the existing system more efficient by means of the Revised Code (Sylvester, 1974, p. 117). An extreme anti-democrat, moreover, he had resolutely opposed any extension of the franchise on the ground that it would merely transfer power 'to those persons who have no sense of decency or morality' (Briggs, op. cit., p. 499). Once the Act was passed, however, he readily set about preparing a scheme for national education, which profoundly influenced W. E. Forster in the formulation of the 1870 Act. He now believed that a national system of education was the country's last defence against anarchy, to be used, as he explained in his lecture on *Primary and Classical Education* (1867), as an instrument with which to teach the working classes to recognize the higher cultivation of their social superiors, for unlike some of his fellow Liberals he could never envisage the Labour aristocracy as allies of the middle classes. Even the 'respectable' National Reform League failed to meet with his approval. 'With such a body', he wrote, 'I have no courtesies to interchange' (ibid.).

Lowe's attitude contrasted diametrically with that of some of his colleagues, particularly the big employers such as Samuel Morley, A. J. Mundella, and W. E. Forster, who had fostered the nascent Lib-Lab alliance. Their view summed up by the 'Rochdale argument' presented an image of a responsible artisan class, eminently suitable as allies for the middle classes, and characterized by self-help, benefit clubs, shares in co-operatives, societies, and an identification with the interests of the capitalist employers. For them the extension of the franchise was therefore an exercise in consolidating the 'respectable' classes against the 'residuum'. For, as Forster explained, the real object of Parliamentary reform was:

> to fight against a class much more dreaded than the holders of the £7 franchise – I mean the dangerous classes in the large towns. If we get into Parliament those who are immediately above them we shall be able to legislate more immediately for them (Harrison, 1965, p. 114).

Forster, nevertheless, still considered it imperative to educate the new electoral class, for as he explained to the Commons on introducing his Elementary Education Bill:

> I am not one of those who would wait until the people were educated before I would trust them with political power. If we had thus waited we might have waited long for education; but now that we have given them political power, we must not wait any longer to give them education (Verbatim Report, p. 18).

In spite of their contrasting views, however, the new situation created by the Act provided a reason for people such as Lowe to co-operate with Forster and his colleagues on the education question.

One further contribution of the Second Reform Act towards the achievement of educational legislation was that it provided Edward Baines and the Voluntaryists with a plausible means of extricating themselves from the difficult position in which their opposition to the government grant had placed them. Consequently, although Baines justified his change of heart in terms of the need to educate the new electorate, his speech to the Congregational Union, in 1867, stressed the great financial difficulties under which his party had been labouring (Maltby, op. cit., p. 102), and its subsequent rapid collapse, particularly in Leeds (Smith, 1931, p. 282), supports the conclusion that it was the inherent problems of Voluntaryism, rather than an expanded electorate, which provided the main motivation for his change of heart. Nevertheless, for the first time since 1843, Radical-Nonconformity could now exert a unified force within the Liberal Party in the cause of national education.

Industry, economic survival and education

As already noted, the American Civil War helped to produce a favourable climate for political reform in Britain. Far less welcome, however, was its creation of an economic colossus to rival her industrial supremacy, the potential of which, as noted in chapter two, had been foreseen by Richard Cobden. 'It is from the West rather than the East that the danger to the supremacy of Great Britain is to be apprehended', he warned in 1835,

> that is from the silent and peaceful rivalry of American commerce, the growth of its manufacturers, its rapid progress, the superior education of its people and their economical and pacific government — it is from these, and not from the barbarous policy and impoverishing armaments of Russia, that the grandeur of our commercial and national prosperity is endangered (Armytage, 1952, p. 207).

Thus it was that the more recent problem of economic survival provided a newer, yet more pressing, reason for national education than the extension of the franchise, equal in gravity to that presented by the urban situation. If the arrival of this new competitor was not portentous enough of Britain's relative economic decline, the Paris Exhibition of 1867 was. Its effect was to initiate a new wave of critical self-examination of British institutions. Here the worst fears of Cobden and Prince Albert, referred to in chapter one, both now deceased, seemed to be confirmed, at least so Lyon Playfair believed. An international juror at the exhibition, he was so shocked at the poor quality of British exhibits that he wrote a long letter of protest to Lord Taunton, then presiding over the Schools Enquiry Commission, claiming not only that Britain had made virtually no progress in 'the peaceful arts of industry' since the previous exhibition in 1862, but that the generally agreed reason for this state of affairs was Britain's lack of 'good systems of industrial education for the masters and managers of factories' possessed by France, Prussia, Belgium and Switzerland (Ashby, 1963, p. 111).

The tale of woe was continued in the report of the Select Committee on Scientific Instruction which had been set up by the Conservatives on Playfair's suggestion. American ingenuity, the Commission was told, was well on the way to surpassing British techniques. Not only had the Americans produced the sewing machine, the reaper, and the centrifugal pump, but also the machine tools which made Nettlefold and Chamberlain's screws and the guns of the Birmingham Small Arms factory. *The Times*, it was revealed, was printed by American presses, John Platt, the owner of the great mechanical engineering empire, admitted that English engineers were in the habit of purchasing American inventions for use in England, and the Birmingham monopoly of the Australian and Canadian hardware markets was being eroded by American goods. Worse still, quite apart from the information given to the Select Committee, it was known that Belgian girders were being used in South

Kensington and Glasgow, and had actually penetrated the very citadel of iron and steel, Sheffield (Armytage, op. cit., pp. 208–9).

As if this were not enough, Germany, on the threshold of unification, constituted another threat, her supremacy in science, technology and scholarship having long been confirmed by the vast numbers of Americans, Englishmen and Continentals who studied at her research-orientated universities. Nor did it go unnoticed that the infra-structure of such a technological empire was a national system of elementary education.

Nobody castigated Britain's lack of system more than that arch-apostle of French and Prussian efficiency Matthew Arnold. In *Schools and Universities on the Continent* (1868), he lamented: 'Our rule of thumb has cost us dear already, and is probably destined to cost us dearer still', its legacy being an education system in disarray, unable to meet the demands of the modern era, particularly the need of scientific advancement:

> The result is that we have to meet the calls of a modern epoch with a working class not educated at all, a middle-class education in the second place, and the idea of science absent from the whole course and design of our education (Arnold, 1868, p. 281).

His panacea for national survival, 'organise your secondary and your superior instruction' (ibid.), clearly had profound implications for elementary education, the ultimate foundation of any education system.

There can be little doubt that the disturbing revelations of the 1860s provided a powerful impetus toward educational legislation. As one American historian has written: 'If the Education Act of 1870 awaited the Reform Act of 1867 it awaited the report of the Select Committee on Scientific Education resulting from the Paris Exhibition of 1867, when British goods were "beaten in everything" ' (Haines, 1959, p. 104). Moreover, the significance of the numerous meetings held in industrial towns in the aftermath of the report in support of improved technical education was not lost on W. E. Forster, as he admitted on introducing his Education Bill:

> Upon the speedy provision of elementary education depends our industrial prosperity. It is no use trying to give technical instruction to our citizens without elementary education . . . and if we leave our work-folk any longer unskilled, notwithstanding their strong sinews and determined energy, they will become over-matched in the competition of the world (Verbatim Report, p. 18).

Knowledge and technical skill, however, were not the only attributes which the school could bequeath to industry. As the Manchester

53

Education Aid Society had argued, children must be prepared for living in an ordered society and for the disciplines demanded by factory work. Now that growing mechanization and the Factory Acts delayed the employment of children, the school was seen to fulfil a crucial preparatory function as the vestibule of the factory. 'The social aspects of this important question especially concern us', stated the Society:

> When for the first ten or twelve years of life there has been no discipline either in life or body . . . is it to be expected that they will quietly and industriously settle down in mills, workshops, warehouses, or at any trade in the orderly routine of any family to work continuously by day, morning and evening, from Monday till Saturday? (Maltby, op. cit., p. 98.)

The answer was clearly in the negative, yet by means of 'the primary education of every child in our great community', such discipline, it was claimed, could be cultivated.

There was yet a further factor which, in addition to those already mentioned, helped to bring the vision of the state-provided school nearer to reality.

The political transformation of Europe and America

If the economic potential of both Europe and North America gave cause for soul-searching, political developments were no less disturbing for those who could comprehend their significance. The victory of the North over the Confederates was seen as the victory of the industrialized, democratized and educated section of the American nation over its agrarian semi-feudal counterpart. Moreover, the military efficiency and power of the North had deeply impressed observers. Similarly, the victory of the Prussian war machine over the Austrians at Sadowa in 1866 gave further cause for reflection upon the power of an efficiently educated soldiery, as John Morley put it: 'The triumphant North of America was the land of the common school. The victory of the Prussians over the Austrians at Sadowa in 1866 was called the victory of the elementary school teacher' (Smith, 1931, p. 282). Perhaps he exaggerated, but what it seemed to demonstrate was that a national system of education was something which modern industrialized states considered indispensable.

These victories had further significance, however. The American industrialists now had the vast potential of the United States at their disposal, and it was only a matter of time before America's political power would be realized. Prussia, meanwhile, in 1870, upon coming into possession of the great industrial and agricultural empire of Imperial

Germany, threw the European balance of power completely out of equilibrium.

It is therefore of little wonder, when faced by such circumstances, that Englishmen, sensitive to their vulnerability, should recognize the need to make the most of the available human resources. The mood was reflected, once again, by Forster:

> Upon this speedy provision of education depends our national power.
> Civilized communities throughout the world are massing themselves
> together, each mass being measured by its force; and if we are to
> hold our position among men of our own race, or among the nations
> of the world, we must make up the smallness of our numbers by in-
> creasing the intellectual force of the individual (Verbatim Report,
> p. 18).

The publication a year later of George Chesney's *Battle of Dorking* (1871), vividly and horrifically describing what might happen if an invading army of Continental stature ever got to grips with Britain's parade-ground soldiery, kept alive the national paranoia.

These were some of the factors which prompted, in the words of Professor Best,

> the unambiguous call, that after thirty and more years of dithering,
> the progress and security of the Nation should cease to be jeopard-
> ized by an elementary system of education so leaky that scores of
> thousands of children who most needed school's civilizing (it was
> hoped) touch, never got near it (Best, 1971, 1973 edn, p. 177).

The response was Forster's Elementary Education Act.

Chapter five

The making of the Elementary Education Act

On his return to power in 1868 at the head of the first truly effective administration since 1846, Gladstone appointed W. E. Forster, Matthew Arnold's brother-in-law and Member for Bradford, as Vice-President of the Committee of Council on Education. The Government, in view of the ferment during the previous twenty years, had a clear mandate to bring in a sweeping educational measure, and as Francis Adams, historian and secretary of the National Education League, wrote in reflection on the period immediately following Palmerston's death:

> The strong current of feeling in favour of a comprehensive law was beginning to be manifested on all occasions throughout society. It was impossible to take up a newspaper or magazine, or to follow the public life of any large town, without discovering how deeply the attention of a part of the community was engaged on the subject (Adams, 1882, 1972 edn, p. 192).

Education accordingly received its due mention in the Queen's speech. The main problem, however, was not whether there ought to be legislation, but what form it should take, and it is for this reason that the standpoints occupied by the various interest groups are so fascinating.

Much was hoped for from Forster, for, as Adams explains, 'he was regarded as the Radical member in the Ministry'. He goes on to describe his interest in the NPSA in the 1850s, and his support of H. A. Bruce's bills of 1867 and 1868, the latter being 'a Free School Bill – the feature of an education programme dearest to Radicalism' (ibid., p. 209). What Adams does not refer to, however, is Forster's suspicion of the extreme Secularist position, as shown in chapter two, merely conceding that Bruce's Education of the Poor Bill was very much a product of the spirit of compromise which had been developing in Manchester since the 1850s.

Bruce's bills, in fact, were the legislative outcome of the foundation of the Manchester Education Bill Committee in 1866 by former members of the Education Aid Society in response to a resolution adopted at a town meeting in Manchester Town Hall on 6 December, demanding a drastic solution to the education problem in the form of 'complete provision for the primary instruction of the children of the poorer classes by means of local rates, under local administration, with legal power in cases of neglect, to enforce attendance at school' (Maltby, 1918, p. 106). Introduced in April 1867 and again the following year by Bruce, Forster and Algernon Egerton, the measure was finally defeated on the question of rate-support for denominational schools. Nevertheless, its importance was considerable, reflecting in its final form the consensus reached at the Manchester Conference of January 1868, attended by a large gathering of educationalists including Lord de Grey, Forster, and Bruce (later to be Liberal Home Secretary), and supported by letters from Kay-Shuttleworth, Lord John Russell, John Stuart Mill, James Bryce, Sir John Pakington, and many other influential people. Briefly it would have empowered districts to support existing voluntary schools and to provide new ones out of the rates. Where deficiencies occurred the Education Department would have been able to compel districts to rate themselves in order to provide schools administered by an elected local authority which, subject to a conscience clause, would have had the power to permit any form of religious teaching.

Clearly this was by no means a secularist measure. It derived from Pakington's Bill of 1857 based on the bill of the Manchester and Salford Committee on Education (ibid., p. 107), which aimed to provide rate support for denominational schools. Therefore, in view of Forster's close involvement with both the 1867 and 1868 versions, Adams's claim that the Radicals could have expected more from him in 1870 was hardly justified (Adams, op. cit., p. 210).

The bill of the Manchester Education Bill Committee was, however, only one of four schemes available for Forster's consideration when he set about drawing up his Elementary Education Bill, for already in Birmingham another more Radical pressure group had been founded, the National Education League.

The National Education League

As we have seen in chapter two, the centre of Radical activity moved from Manchester to Birmingham in 1857 (page 25). In the Midland town municipal pride and educational achievement were closely related, the leaders of the education movement being also the leaders of the Birmingham municipal reform movement, having been inspired by the teaching of the Unitarian minister, George Dawson, on the civilizing role of municipal authorities. Typical of such people was William Harris, a founder member of Dawson's congregation, architect and surveyor, some time President of the Birmingham Liberal Association and formerly Hon. Secretary of the Birmingham branch of the National Public School Association.

Harris was convinced of the need to establish representative institutions for the purpose of raising funds for elementary schools, the initial outcome being the Birmingham Education Society (Hennock, 1973, p. 81). Modelled on the Manchester Education Aid Society, it was founded in 1867 at the house of George Dixon, a wealthy merchant recently recruited to the Town Council and in his year of mayoralty. Dixon became president of the new body, and the Hon. Secretary was Jesse Collings, an ironmonger and another member of Dawson's church, who had originally persuaded Dixon to take an initiative on education on the Manchester model.

Most energetic of all, however, and perhaps the most exciting politician of the late nineteenth century, was Joseph Chamberlain. Head of the commercial side of the screw manufacturing firm of Nettlefold and Chamberlain, a Unitarian and a Sunday School teacher, he, according to the testimony of a friend, 'far surpassed in ability any previous local leaders' (Briggs, 1972, p. XVI). Chamberlain, in fact, was to the Birmingham movement what Cobden had been to the Anti-Corn Law League, providing the drive and political acumen. Curiously enough, however, it was the more moderate Dixon who most resembled Cobden in his approach to the education question.

By July 1868, with the failure of the local Education Society to provide a Voluntaryist answer to the education question, it had become obvious in Birmingham, as in Manchester, that a more drastic solution involving rate-aid was required. Collings seized the initiative. Returning to the uncompromising position of the Manchester Radicals in the 1850s, he advocated the adoption of the Massachusetts Common School system in a pamphlet entitled *An Outline of the American system with remarks on the establishment of common schools in England* (1868), having taken his information from the Rev. James Fraser's report to the Taunton Commission (Armytage, 1970, p. 124 n). He proposed the immediate formation of a society to promote a programme of 'national secular education, compulsory as to rating and attendance, with state aid and inspection and local management' (Hennock, op. cit., p. 86), the result being the foundation of the National Education League, modelled like its Manchester predecessor, the NPSA, on the Anti-Corn Law League. Tightly controlled from its Birmingham headquarters, the new organization swiftly went into action, holding lecture meetings, producing pamphlets and issuing a journal, the *Monthly Paper*; activities which by February 1869 had produced 2500 members, and by the following year 113 branches, a guarantee fund of £60,000 and a steady income of £6000 per year. Such strong financial support reflects the powerful backing of local Liberalism which the NPSA, being the product of an unpopular faction, had never enjoyed to the same extent in Manchester. Moreover, whereas the latter had never been strongly represented on the town council, the League, by the end of 1869, had eleven members on the Birmingham council, including Collings and Chamberlain, the latter thereby beginning his distinguished political career by way of the education movement.

The League also enjoyed the support of organized Labour to an extent that the NPSA had never achieved, many trade unionists coming in straight from the National Reform League, the most distinguished of these being Robert Applegarth, Secretary of the Amalgamated Society of Carpenters and Joiners, who became an executive committee member. He was also a friend of A. J. Mundella, Forster's successor at the Education Department, and had collected information on Swiss education for Forster when attending the Basle Congress of the International Working Men's Association in 1869 (McCann, 1970, p. 136). Another similarly influential Labour member was George Howell, the former Secretary of the Reform League. Public meetings for working men were held in many large towns, but in addition Working Men's Auxiliaries, *ad hoc* bodies of artisans, of which there were fifteen, did a great deal of useful work on the League's behalf.

The Manchester antecedents of the League were certainly not lost on George Dixon, its chairman, nor on Francis Adams, who informs his readers of Dixon's generous comment in recognition of the earlier work of Cobden and the NPSA:

> Had my suggestions been favourably received by the gentleman to whom they were made, Birmingham would not have originated the League, but would have followed Manchester, which in my opinion ought to have headed, and was entitled to lead, a national movement (Adams, op. cit., p. 195).

It is most unlikely, however, that the chauvinistic Chamberlain would have permitted Birmingham to defer to Manchester in this way. In the event the issue did not arise, for despite the formation of the League branch in Manchester, the former NPSA members, such as the Rev. Dr William McKerrow, Dr W. B. Hodgson and others, were happy to hand over the initiative to Birmingham (ibid., p. 199). Moreover, despite pronouncements by Jacob Bright and George Dixon in support of the harmony of interests between the League and the Manchester Education Bill Committee, the two bodies remained separate (Maltby, op. cit., p. 113).

The National Education Union

As if to emphasize the rivalry between the two towns, a recurrent theme in the nineteenth century, Manchester now became the centre of a new pressure group, the National Education Union, founded in August 1869, with a branch in Birmingham. As Francis Adams complained, its main purpose was to obstruct the League's secular programme in order to preserve the denominational schools; an opinion which James Fraser, the former Newcastle Assistant Commissioner and future Bishop of Manchester, corroborated as follows at a Union meeting in the Free Trade Hall in 1870: 'I suppose if it had not been for the existence of the Education League and the programme they put forth, the Education Union, which has assembled us here tonight, would have had no existence' (Adams, op. cit., p. 208).

In great contrast to the League, which was Liberal and Nonconformist in character, the Union was very much a Tory—Anglican organization, notwithstanding the adhesion of Liberals such as Edward Baines and Cowper-Temple. For example, among its 578 vice-presidents in 1870 were two Archbishops, five Dukes, one Marquis, eighteen Earls, twenty-one Bishops, twenty-one Barons, and 111 MPs, eliciting the comment from Francis Adams that 'while the League could hardly boast a coronet, the Union(s) had little else to boast of' (ibid., p. 207). Briefly, it aimed to extend the voluntary system by means of rates and taxes, to ensure the perpetuation of the government grant to voluntary schools, to counteract the efforts of the League, and to secure the return of MPs sympathetic to the teaching of denominational religion in schools. Moreover, whatever Francis Adams might have thought, the Union enjoyed the support of the inert mass of conservative opinion. It was, therefore, the rallying point of the supporters of the existing system, having, in consequence, no need to draft new legislation, but merely to defend the *status quo*. The League, on the other hand, like the Anti-Corn Law League and the NPSA before it, was obliged to go on the attack, readily incurring charges of irreligion when advocating the secular schools which were the crux of its proposed national system. The juxtaposition of these two pressure groups, therefore, on the eve of the passing of the Elementary Education Act, epitomized the problem of educational reform in the nineteenth century.

Ironically enough, despite its patrician associations, the Union was not devoid of working-class support, and seems actually to have won the race with the League in setting up the first Working Men's Auxiliary in Birmingham (McCann, op. cit., p. 139). Nevertheless, the Labour movement in the Midland town predominantly supported the Secularists. In Manchester, by contrast, Labour was sharply divided between the rival factions, leading to the violent breaking up of working-men's league meetings in the Town Hall on 11 March and later in Salford (ibid., p. 141). The League's energetic supporters, however, ensured that its principles were well known in the organized labour movement, and probably commanded its support on all the issues involved, with the possible exception of Bible reading in schools, to which the League was opposed. In Robert Applegarth's opinion, at least, working men were largely indifferent to this issue, the religious difficulty in education having been created for the working classes, not by them (ibid., p. 146). It is worth noting that this opinion was shared by the Newcastle Commission.

Robert Lowe's scheme

Robert Lowe provided the fourth plan available to Forster, the elements of which he had described in his lecture, *Primary and Classical Education*, delivered in Edinburgh in November 1867. Characteristically, he argued that the state had a duty to guard the constitution against the 'evil' of democracy by implementing 'the most universal measure of education that could be devised'. He therefore envisaged a compulsory, locally-controlled system, judged in terms of results as under current practice and, in view of the state's involvement, strictly secular in content. It was to be initiated by a survey of every parish in order to assess the level of deficiency, after which the Privy Council would give notice to the parishes to provide the necessary schools. In contrast with the plan of the National Education League, existing schools would remain undisturbed except for the obligation to submit to undenominational inspection and a conscience clause. Parishes refusing to act could be forced by the government to levy a compulsory rate for school provision, and all new schools would benefit from existing grants through the system of payment by results. Small wonder is it, in view of Lowe's emphasis on the secular content of the curriculum, that Francis Adams should label him 'the most able minister who has yet held the post of vice-president' (Adams, op. cit., p. 169), a description which for reasons which will become evident he was unwilling to accord to Forster.

Forster's memorandum

Although Gladstone formed his ministry in December 1868, Forster was unable to bring his elementary education bill forward until the bill to disestablish the Irish Church had been disposed of and he had placed the Endowed Schools Act safely on the Statute Book. Moreover, to complicate matters even further, in the same year, 1869, he was also obliged to deal with an outbreak of cattle pest (Reid, 1888, I, p. 450), a symptom of the polyglot nature of the responsibilities which the

Privy Council embraced and which periodically arrived on the Vice-President's doorstep.

However, on 21 October, he produced a draft entitled 'Memorandum by Mr Forster of suggestions for consideration in framing the Education Bill for England', Gladstone having already shown an interest in expediting matters, notwithstanding Bruce's statement that national education was the 'one subject on which Uncle William did not seem well up and interested' (Vincent, 1966, 1972 edn, p. 255). In view of the fact that the memorandum was subsequently changed, leaving Forster's bill with a weaker rationale than the original draft would have provided, it is worth examining closely.

Aims The memorandum explained that the education system needed to be changed because voluntary efforts were not giving the nation the 'complete national system' that it required (Reid, op. cit., p. 464). Forster's twin aim, therefore, was 'to cover the country with good schools' and 'to get the parents to send their children to school', bearing in mind the principles that there should be the least possible expenditure of public money, and the least possible injury to efficient schools, the object being not to replace the existing system but 'to fill up the gaps'. The virtues of family responsibility, self-help and economy were, therefore, to remain sacrosanct wherever possible.

Of the four plans available to Forster, he found that of the National Education Union to be 'insufficient'. The League's scheme, on the other hand, went too far, threatening 'to drive out of the field most of those who care for education, and oblige the government to make use solely of official or municipal agency' (ibid., p. 466). As for the Manchester scheme, in spite of his former support for Bruce's bill, Forster now drew back from compelling ratepayers to provide rate-aid for voluntary schools and turned instead to Lowe's plan, 'the ruling idea of which . . . (was) compulsory school provision, if and where necessary, but not otherwise' (ibid.). The extent of educational need, in accordance with Lowe's suggestion, was to be ascertained by dividing the country up into school districts from which returns of educational deficiency would be made. If a deficient district then refused to rate itself, the government would 'possibly' have the power to act in its stead (Roper, 1973, p. 66). By this means, those who preferred the existing system would have the opportunity to keep it, 'but their preference and dislike would not be allowed to keep a district in destitution' (Reid, op. cit., p. 467).

Despite the credit given by Forster to Lowe, the memorandum was very much an amalgam of principles which had been continually debated over the last twenty years, including some of his own. The idea of 'filling up the gaps' revealed by a survey had appeared in W. J. Fox's bill of 1850, and had later been suggested to the Select Committee on Education in 1865 by R. R. W. Lingen. Compulsory provision, meanwhile, had been an important provision of Bruce's bill of 1868. Moreover, when he came to discuss the powers which were to be granted to the rate-payers over the existing voluntary schools and the new state-provided schools, Forster, in his determination to enable the localities to extend rate-aid to the voluntary schools, moved away from Lowe back to the Manchester-inspired standpoint of Bruce's bill. He therefore proposed to permit them to be supported out of the rates, provided that the money was spent exclusively on secular instruction, the entire cost of religious instruction being met solely by the voluntary body. The new rate-provided schools, however, being state schools, were to be forbidden to teach denominational religion for, argued Forster, it would be unfair 'to tax a Roman Catholic to teach Methodism' (ibid.), whereas it would not be unfair to 'levy a rate on a Roman Catholic for the secular education of a Methodist' (ibid., p. 468). Thus by stressing that the rates were to be spent only on the teaching of secular knowledge, Forster hoped to grant rate-aid to voluntary schools without 'putting religion on the rates'.

Logically, according to this rationale, religious instruction should have been completely excluded from the rate-provided schools, but, as already noted, Forster was no Secularist and was determined that they should be avowedly Christian establishments. He therefore proposed that they should all teach undenominational religious instruction, a practice advocated by the League and similar to that operating in Massachusetts.

As for the problems of attendance, Forster showed that he had moved away from his previous belief that it could be enforced indirectly by the Factory Acts and proposed, in anticipation of the scheme implemented by Lord Sandon in 1876, to make the parents' duty to educate their children a legal obligation, enforcible 'by officials . . . appointed by the rate-payers' (ibid., p. 469).

The importance of this memorandum lies in the fact that had its rationale been incorporated into the Elementary Education Bill the government would have been in a far better position than it eventually was to defend itself against the onslaught of its own alienated Non-conformist supporters on the issues of rate-aid for voluntary schools and compulsory attendance. Unfortunately, the concept of unsectarian religious instruction was anathema to the High Anglican Gladstone for whom theological purity held first priority. He therefore insisted on either allowing the new schools to teach denominational religious instruction or no religion at all (Roper, op. cit., p. 69). Knowing that a secular bill would have had little chance of success, Forster was obliged to accept the first alternative and permit the new school boards, provided in the bill for the purpose of managing the rate-supported schools, to 'be left in the same position as managers of voluntary schools' (Verbatim Report, p. 14), and to spend the ratepayers' money on denominational religious teaching if they so wished. He thus found himself with no alternative but to stir up the Nonconformist hornets' nest by threatening to subsidize denominational religious instruction from the rates. Furthermore, in order to avert Tory—Anglican opposition and thus increase the bill's chances of survival, the provision for universal compulsory attendance was dropped by the Cabinet in favour of a permissive measure, enabling individual school boards to enforce attendance if they so wished. Unhappily, this flirtation with the 'art of the possible' was to have unpleasant repercussions for the Liberal Party in the succeeding months.

The progress of the bill

In spite of these difficulties, Forster introduced his bill on 17 February 1870 amid general acclaim, Sir John Pakington and Cowper-Temple, chairman of the National Education Union, both speaking enthusiastically in its favour. Even George Dixon, the League Chairman, agreed that the promise in the Queen's speech was 'now fully redeemed'. The press, meanwhile, hailed it with a chorus of approbation (Reid, op. cit., p. 480).

Briefly, it proposed to give voluntary bodies a year in which to supply existing educational need, after which any deficiencies would be provided by a school board, elected by the town council in boroughs and by the vestry in country districts, with the duty either of providing new schools from rate-aid or helping existing schools (Verbatim Report, p. 13). As already stated, this matter and that of religious instruction were left to the boards to decide for themselves, provided there was a conscience clause and that all schools were assisted on equal terms. The boards also could enforce the attendance of children between the ages of five and eleven if they so wished.

The honeymoon period in the aftermath of the First Reading was, alas, all too short. In Parliament the Anglican Dixon might speak in statesmanlike manner, but the voice of Birmingham and the League belonged to Chamberlain who, like the Anti-Corn Law Leaguers and some of the NPSA members before him, saw the educational struggle as merely a phase in the greater campaign for the disestablishment of the Anglican Church. The reaction which the bill met in Birmingham was, therefore, very different from that at Westminster, and when a League delegation met Gladstone on 9 March, Chamberlain made a strong impression on him much to the discomfiture of both Forster and his successor, A. J. Mundella, the latter writing ominously to his friend, Leader, editor of the *Sheffield Telegraph*, 'The Secularists in the League are pushing the Nonconformists into antagonism about the religious question' (Armytage, 1951, p. 78). He was quite right, for

already, a week before, a Central Nonconformist Co
set up in Birmingham in order to fan the flames
opposition to rate-support for the Anglican dom
schools. Presided over by the Congregationalist min
and the Unitarian Rev. H. W. Crosskey, it was very m
of Cobden's organization of the pro-disestablishmer
ministers in support of the Anti-Corn Law League a
tury before. Meanwhile, as Forster's biographer informs us, he knew
that his refusal to 'employ education as a stalking horse, by means of
which to attack the Established Church', was a grievous disappointment
to the Nonconformists (Reid, op. cit., p. 481), yet he steadfastly
adhered to the position which he held since 1850, which was simply to
obtain rate-support for elementary education by whatever means possible. As he wrote to Charles Kingsley when the menacing forces of the
League, the Nonconformists and the Bradford 'caucus' were gathering
about him:

> I still fully believe that I shall get my bill through this year, but I
> wish parsons, Church, and *other*, would all remember as much as
> you do that children are growing into savages while they are trying
> to prevent one another from helping them (ibid., p. 491).

Appropriately, it was this very situation that *Punch* portrayed in the
now famous cartoon on 26 March 1870, entitled 'The Three Rs; OR,
Better late than never'.

By this time the League, with its 113 branches in support, had decided to go to the unusual lengths of opposing the bill's Second Reading,
and mounted a campaign in opposition to several of its provisions,
notably the year's grace, during which the voluntary bodies could try
'to fill up the gaps', the failure to provide universal school boards and
compulsory attendance, the conscience clause which Nonconformists
had always claimed to be ineffective and, finally, the power of the
school boards to support voluntary schools from the rates and establish denominational board schools.

The amended bill

The result of all this furore was that Gladstone, having been obliged to
meet another deputation on 11 April, this time from the Central Nonconformist Committee, at last awoke to the intensity of opposition
from Bradford and Birmingham, the brunt of which Forster had hitherto borne. In a letter to Lord Granville he wrote:

> I am loath to trouble you with a quarter of an hour's reading, but

ne subject of Education is so important and so arduous in regard to the 'religious difficulty' that I am perhaps justified in attempting this infliction (Briggs, op. cit., p. xxxi).

The outcome was a whole series of amendments designed to make the bill more acceptable, the most important of which were introduced by Gladstone when the House went into committee on 16 June. The first and most ironic, in view of Gladstone's antipathy to non-sectarian religious instruction, was Cowper-Temple's amendment forbidding the teaching in board schools of any 'catechism or formulary' distinctive of any particular denomination (Verbatim Report, p. 152). The second, accepted by the Cabinet on Robert Lowe's suggestion, denied rate-support to the voluntary schools in return for an increased exchequer grant of 50 per cent, thus founding the 'dual system' in English education: voluntary schools and local authority schools existing side by side but under separate control. Third, Gladstone proposed to abolish the building grant which, since its inception in 1833, had been virtually monopolized by the Church. Yet this was by no means the devastating blow at Anglican domination that it might seem, for as he explained to the House:

> The building of schools is the easiest of all the efforts made by the promoters. Their greatest difficulty is the maintenance of their schools; and when we give liberal assistance to the maintenance, I think we may fairly leave to the locality the cost of building (ibid., p. 155).

The League received a severe mauling during the committee stage of the bill, suffering defeats over their proposals for free, compulsory education and the supply of religious instruction by voluntary agencies. Unfortunately, some prominent Liberals were involved in these defeats and the situation was aggravated by the support received by the government from the Opposition, which ensured that in spite of the disaffection of the Nonconformists, the government always had a majority. Particularly aggrieved were Edward Miall, Forster's co-member for Bradford, and Henry Richards, MP for Merthyr Tydfil. 'They laughed who won', lamented Miall, for the Church, he alleged, had received all that it deserved, while the Nonconformists had been made to pass through the 'Valley of Humiliation', betrayed by a government which owed its position to the Nonconformist votes (ibid., p. 505). Richards similarly declared that the Act was being forced upon the country in the teeth of Nonconformist opposition, despite the fact that they represented half the nation and more than half the Liberal Party (ibid., p. 543).

The Act, which finally received the Royal Assent on 9 August, did not represent by any means a capitulation to the Church. In addition to the amendments already noted, the period of grace during the Committee Stage had been reduced to six months, an amendment to make the reading of the Bible compulsory was refused and the proposal to elect the school boards by ballot was carried against Tory opposition after an all-night sitting. Furthermore, the nature of the boards themselves was changed. Instead of being appointed by local councils, as originally proposed, they were redesigned on the lines of the American school committees; *ad hoc* bodies elected directly by the ratepayers, on a broad franchise, solely for the purpose of providing elementary education and, for this reason, potentially very Radical in urban centres.

The Church, nevertheless, had received enough to enable the voluntary schools to survive until they were at last granted rate-support in 1902, and moreover, the notorious Clause 25, permitting boards to pay the school pence of poor children, still, in spite of amendments, enabled the ratepayers' money to be spent on denominational schools. It was for this that the extreme Nonconformists could not forgive Forster.

The Forster Act was in many ways an unsatisfactory measure. In establishing the 'dual system' in elementary education it perpetuated, in the impecunious voluntary schools denied of rate-support, an impediment to educational progress, the repercussions of which are felt even today. It provided neither universally obligatory nor free education, leaving the matter of compulsory attendance to the discretion of the school boards and confining free education to the very poor. Even the boards themselves were not established everywhere, being created only where there was a deficiency of accommodation, or at the behest of the ratepayers in boroughs and parishes. Nevertheless, as a collectivist measure, it represents a crucial change in the role of the state, marking the point at which it was transformed from the mere stimulation of the educational efforts of others to the assumption of direct responsibility for educating the nation's children. The basic foundation of a national system of universal, free, compulsory education had at last been laid. As Professor Armytage has written: 'This was the most efficient factory act yet passed, for it did bring the children into schools for part of their lives' (Armytage, 1951, p. 80).

Chapter six

Compulsory education

The aftermath of the Education Act

The Act had a devastating effect on the Liberals, and undoubtedly contributed to their defeat in the election of 1874. The League, meanwhile, remained in existence until 1877, opposing its provisions, determined that Forster should never forget his 'betrayal' of his Nonconformist origins.

Forster's determination to place his Act on the Statute Book, in spite of the onslaught of the League faction, nevertheless evokes a certain admiration. A radical industrialist, typical of what John Vincent calls 'the heroic element' in Parliamentary Liberalism (Vincent, 1966, 1972 edn, p. 73), he was one of those who provided an 'element of distinct purpose' within the party (ibid.), one of thirty or forty great capitalists who, through lifelong commitment to a particular cause, provided the Liberal drive for humanitarian reform. Other members of this group, all of whom were extremely powerful in their own localities, were Bass the Burton brewer, Titus Salt, creator of the Saltaire factory community near Bradford, and Hugh Mason, the Ashton-under-Lyne cotton manufacturer.

Forster's own personal eminence in the West Riding, however, did not save him from the wrath of the Bradford party 'caucus'. In a crowded meeting in St George's Hall shortly after the Act had been passed, he was accused of legislating for the majority of the nation and, consequently, against the interests of his own supporters; a charge framed, ironically, as an amendment to a vote of thanks for his services to the town. As his biographer informs us, perhaps a little over-sentimentally, the 'ammunition of Birmingham had been imported to Bradford for the purpose of wounding its distinguished representative in his own political home' (Reid, 1888, I, p. 519).

The Liberal intelligentsia were no more enchanted with the Act than the Nonconformists. J. S. Mill complained:

A more effectual plan could have scarcely been devised by the strongest champion of ecclesiastical ascendancy for enabling the clergy of the Church of England to indoctrinate the children of the greater part of England and Wales in their religion at the expense of the public (Adams, 1882, 1972 edn, p. 236).

T. H. Green, idealist philosopher and League member, meanwhile, objected to Forster's failure to provide universal school boards and compulsory attendance. The establishment of small inefficient rural boards, and the perpetuation of the 'unjust and in a sense demoralising' denominational system, also irked him (Nettleship, ed., 1906, pp. 111, 436–45), yet significantly he was full of praise for the work of the larger boards.

Such complaints, however, were mild compared with the invective of John Morley, Mill's Lancashire-born literary protégé, editor of the *Fortnightly Review*, and champion of Nonconformity (Hamer, 1968, p. 96). Through him the disappointments of the Nonconformists found their clearest expression. Education, in Morley's view, was 'the most serious of national causes', equivalent in importance as a contemporary Radical issue to the repeal of the Corn Laws in the 1840s and, appropriately enough for one who had placed his journal at the disposal of Joseph Chamberlain, his pamphlet, *The Struggle for National Education* (1873), has been described as the 'single indispensable polemic' of the protracted debate (Briggs, 1972, p. xliii).

Morley was convinced that in 1870 the Liberals had lost a great opportunity to bring about a 'thorough settlement' of the education question based on the principle of religious equality on which, he alleged, 'the ministerial majority had been returned' (Morley, 1873, p. 12). The Liberal victory, he argued, should have yielded a rich harvest for the Nonconformists. Yet instead, not only had the results been bitterly disappointing, but they had actually worked to the advantage of the Anglican Church. With an Act 'which a Conservative Chamber would not have rejected', Forster had given the denominational system the most valuable help that it had ever had and, 'as if to compensate the Anglican Church for the loss of prestige she had sustained by Irish disestablishment', he had done his best 'to hand over to her the elementary education of England' (ibid., p. 14). He was particularly incensed by the damage caused within the party, the supreme irony being that whereas 'Mr Disraeli had had the satisfaction of dishing the Whigs, who were his enemies, Mr Gladstone, on the other hand, dished the dissenters who were his friends' (ibid., p. 15).

The political dimension was only one aspect of the problem, however, for like Cobden and Prince Albert before him, Morley considered education to be nothing less than a matter of national survival. He clearly recognized that American and German industrial competition put the uninstructed workman at a growing disadvantage, making 'rude vigour, undisciplined by intellectual training' no longer sufficient to meet the demands of modern economic circumstances. Even the rude and vigorous Australians had seen the disadvantages of 'brute ignorance in an age of cultivated skill'. Consequently, while England temporized with her 'dual system' the state of Victoria, by the Act of 1872, had taken education out of the hands of the religious organizations and established a compulsory, free, secular system of elementary education which England, he argued, would be wise to emulate, for under her existing system even the constitution was at stake: 'In plain English, a majority of those who come out of schools cannot read a newspaper. This unfortunate class is our ruling class.'

One is hardly surprised to note, in view of his League affiliation, that Morley's considered solution to these problems was the implementation of an education system which was free, secular, compulsory and controlled by universal school boards (ibid., pp. 110ff.).

The Victoria Act, 1872

Morley's reference to the Victoria Act of 1872 gives rise to the question of why an Australian state legislature could pass an act which would have gladdened the hearts of the National Education League, while England had to be content with the 'dual system'. As an Australian historian has recently suggested (Zainu'ddin, 1964, pp. 58–83), in a densely populated country like England, where centralization was suspect and the tradition of local control established, a decentralized education system composed of a variety of state and voluntary schools was feasible; a solution which was out of the question in sparsely populated Victoria, where, in the words of one inspector, 'local communities tended to be composed of ignorant men, in every way unfit for the control of teachers' (ibid., p. 81). Second, whereas Forster and his fellow MPs, ever conscious of the need for economy, were legislating for the 'lower orders', the less socially elevated Victorian Parliament was legislating for the children of its own members and was, consequently, eager to undertake the expense of a centralized system. The predominant factor, however, was the relative weight of tradition and the past which, while leaving the Australians untrammelled, impeded the mother country with a history of sectarian strife dating back to the seventeenth century.

Viewed in this light, Forster, in spite of Morley's criticism, seems to have had little room for manoeuvre in 1870. Not that the Nonconformists saw the situation in the same light. Encouraged by the repeal of the Corn Laws in 1846 and Gladstone's disestablishment of the Irish Church in 1869, they were eager for further victories and ultimately the demise of the Church of England, hence their bitter disappointment at his refusal to promote its obliteration by means of an education act. They could hardly be blamed for misreading the course of history and failing to see that in thirty-two years' time, the Church, far from disintegrating, would still be influential enough to persuade a Conservative Government to put its denominational schools on the rates through the Education Act of 1902.

An electoral system in microcosm

Morley took a very jaundiced view of the possibilities for elementary education under the Act. Yet already the edifice, which was eventually to provide a quality of education scarcely envisaged in 1870, had been established. As already noted, the boards were bodies whose sole purpose, in the absence of an articulated system of local government administration, was to supply existing deficiencies in elementary education, having no other function. They were not established universally, but only where a majority of ratepayers voted to establish a board. They were, moreover, very democratic in constitution, closely imitating the Massachusetts school committees beloved by the League and the NPSA before it, and having a wide franchise which permitted both men and women to vote and stand for election.

By far their most curious feature, however, was the system of cumulative voting, introduced during the committee stage, which enabled minority groups to be represented, each elector being allowed to cast as many votes as there were board members. This number varied between five and fifteen according to the size of the school district, except in the case of London, which originally had forty-nine and, after 1882, fifty-five members. A voter was then enabled either to spread his votes or to use them all in support of a single individual. Francis Adams and other League members complained bitterly about this system, and George Dixon later introduced a bill to amend it, but without success. He had good reason, because at the first school board election in Birmingham the Liberals put up fifteen candidates, of whom only six were elected, to be faced with eight 'conservatives and churchmen' and a Roman Catholic priest who had come top of the poll (Adams, op. cit., pp. 49ff.). Priests, as a result of the cumulative vote, did well in any area where there was a sizeable Catholic community, even invading Rochdale, the stronghold of the Quaker, John Bright, much to his horror (Reid, op. cit., p. 527).

Plumping, as the cumulative vote was known, nevertheless remained and, as Adams indicates, promoted the development of the party 'caucus' in the constituencies as a result of the need to organize the electorate for the triennial board elections. The Birmingham Liberals, meanwhile, profiting from the examples of their Bradford colleagues, organized their votes so successfully in subsequent elections that they were able to command a majority until the late 1890s. The secret ballot was not universally enforced until 1872, so that board elections sometimes exhibited 'every description of trickery, deception and fraud' (Adams, op. cit., p. 251). As a correspondent from Kendal wrote, 'I have seen something of voting in half civilized states, but Mr Forster's School Board voting has no equal in fostering falsehood and trickery' (ibid.).

One very important effect of the establishment of the boards was to move much of the religious controversy from the centre to the periphery of the educational system, a consequence which was not entirely unintended (Sutherland, 1973, p. 93), and the acrimony engendered was often considerable enough to convince Francis Adams that 'no parliamentary or local controversy had for generations previously been known to provoke the same bitterness and division between the parties' (Adams, op. cit., p. 251). The board elections, nevertheless, provided an indispensable vehicle for developing techniques of organizing the mass electorate which developed as the result of successive extensions of the franchise after the Reform Act of 1867, and their contribution to the democratic process in providing a system of participatory democracy cannot be overestimated.

The school boards

The school boards, therefore, were the first democratically-elected, local-education authorities, numbering, by 1871, about 300. The London board, because of its size, progressive nature and distinguished membership, inevitably provided a model for others to follow. Composed of such eminent individuals as Lord Lawrence, former Viceroy of India, Professor T. H. Huxley, Elizabeth Garrett Anderson, Emily Davies, Lord Sandon and W. H. Smith, the stationer, it amply justified the statement in *The Times* of 29 November 1870 that 'no equally powerful body will exist in England outside Parliament if power be influence for good or evil over masses of human beings'. It also appeared to illustrate the anxiety of the voters 'to elect thoroughly efficient members . . . (rather) than to secure the triumph of a particular dogma, religious or political'.

Birmingham also manifested the willingness of its leading citizens to take local government seriously. The board included industrialists like Sampson Lloyd and A. J. Elkington, politicians such as Chamberlain and Dixon, the Rev. F. S. Dale, the Anglican voluntary-school leader, and the Congregationalist the Rev. R. W. Dale, successor to the Rev. George Dawson as Birmingham's Nonconformist conscience. Sheffield was equally well served by Skelton Cole, the draper, and the industrialists Charles Doncaster, Henry Wilson, Mark Firth and Sir John Brown; a pattern of response which was repeated in Manchester, Liverpool and other large industrial towns.

Undoubtedly, therefore, one of the most important functions that the school boards performed was to bring influential people such as these face to face with social problems which had previously been known to only a few, thereby increasing the social awareness of the community at large. The boards' own journal, *The School Board Chronicle*, of 22 April 1871, put the matter succinctly:

It appears that the persons who will undergo the strictest process
of education are the members of the School Boards themselves.
... Already there are several hundred gentlemen and a few ladies,
whose minds are now devoted to the subject of education as a reality.
They are brought face to face with all sorts of ideas to which they
have been strangers, or which they have previously shirked. ... They
have had to meet, work with and treat with respect all sorts of
people whom they have previously shunned (Sturt, 1967, p. 315).

A report of the clerk to the Sheffield School Board provides a vivid example of the 'shunned', who had now become the daily concern of the school boards. Describing the conditions in which an impoverished family, deserted by the father, were living, he went on:

A more miserable picture of squalid misery it is impossible to
conceive; scarcely a whole pane remained in the windows; there
was no food in the house; and as the mother refused to take her
family into the workhouse, it is left to the Officers of the Board to
enforce the attendance of the children at school (Bingham, 1949,
p. 63).

As the statement reveals, the Sheffield board, in common with most of the large urban boards, was employing school attendance officers or 'visitors'; a new professional group, created by the school boards who were often the subject of scorn and contempt. Nevertheless they gathered together such an invaluable mass of information on urban poverty that when Charles Booth was compiling his survey on the London poor at the end of the century he was moved to write: 'Taking them as a body I cannot feel too highly of their ability and good sense . . . without [their help] nothing could have been done' (Rubinstein, 1969, p. 53). In fact it was these people who provided the shock troops in the battle for attendance which was begun under the permissive clauses of the Forster Act.

The larger boards were generally very energetic indeed in carrying out their obligations, particularly with regard to the enforcement of attendance. Their size, however, made them the exception rather than the rule, 75 per cent of the boards having only the minimum of five members and a quarter of them being responsible for a population of less than 500 each. Such bodies, mostly in rural areas, impoverished and dominated by local farmers, often acted as a brake on education, being more interested in keeping down the rates than providing schools. Cheshire's record was particularly notorious. Not only were its rural boards extremely retrogressive, but in Stockport it possessed the only sizeable town in the country to succeed in dissolving its school board. Moreover, so abhorrent were the school boards to the inhabitants of Birkenhead that they raised £17,500 by a voluntary rate in order to avoid having one (Rogers, 1970–1, pp. 51–62).

It was, in fact, the alleged inefficiency of the smaller boards which brought the system into disrepute and provided some of the ammunition for those who wished to destroy them at the end of the century. Even Fabian Socialists like Sidney Webb who admired the work of the larger boards saw the need to replace the smaller ones with larger authorities (Brennan, 1975, p. 52). Yet the educational work went on and between 1870 and 1902 the battle for attendance was won, but not without the help of further legislation, support for which came, as will be seen below, from a rather unusual quarter.

The demand for compulsory attendance

The desire to make school attendance compulsory did not originate in the period immediately prior to the passing of Forster's Act, having been advocated in the 1830s by those admirers of Continental bureaucracy, A. J. Roebuck and other Radical MPs. In the 1850s, however, the NPSA, believing that school pence was the great overriding obstacle in the way of universal school attendance, omitted compulsory provision from their plan. It is noteworthy, however, that the Rev. Dr William McKerrow, one of the Association's most active workers and a future member of the Manchester School Board, expressing a collectivist viewpoint before the Select Committee on Manchester and Salford Education, hinted at the possible need for compulsory measures should parents refuse to send their children to school, adding, 'I do not see any right that any individual has to bring up his children to be a nuisance to society' (Hinton, 1854, p. 90). Six years previously, in his *Principles of Political Economy* (1848), John Stuart Mill had written, 'It is . . . an allowable exercise of the powers of government to impose on parents the legal obligation of giving elementary instruction to their children' (Sutherland, op. cit., p. 118). The education of children, therefore, according to this argument, was far too important a matter to be left to the individual parent to decide upon. It was responsibility to be enforced by the state.

The revelations of the Education Aid Society in the 1860 any illusion that the removal of school pence would automati about mass elementary education. Consequently, as already n the Manchester Education Bill Committee and the National Education League pressed Forster to make attendance universally compulsory. Moreover, all the HMIs who reported on attendance in 1869 considered it necessary (ibid.). Since 1833, however, various groups of children had been made subject to indirect compulsory provision by the Factory, Mines and Workshop Acts, which limited their working hours and required them to spend a stipulated number of hours at school, but these were not very effective and applied to a very small number of children. Nor was Denison's Act of 1855, which permitted the Poor Law Guardians to make regular school attendance a condition of out-door relief to parents, any more effective.

It was, in fact, the knowledge of this situation which had persuaded Forster, previously a supporter of indirect compulsion, to urge the adoption of methods of a more direct nature in his first memorandum. As already noted, the Cabinet would only agree to make compulsion a permissive measure, enforceable at the discretion of the boards, but in 1872, in response to pressure from both wings of the Liberal Party, symbolized in the 'Bristol platform', Forster stated his intention of bringing in a measure which would have made attendance enforceable in non-school board districts by Boards of Guardians. He also intended to transfer to them the delicate business of paying the school fees of poor children, thereby taking the heat out of Clause 25 of the Education Act, which had originally assigned this controversial function to the school boards. Unfortunately, no sooner had he obtained the agreement of the Cabinet than Gladstone decided upon his abortive resignation of 1873, only to find that the Conservatives could not form a ministry.

A further attempt to legislate in the next year was forestalled by Gladstone's final enigmatic dissolution in February 1874, throwing the Liberals into complete disarray. The succeeding catastrophic Liberal defeat, meanwhile, ensured that Forster would be prevented from completing the edifice which he had done so much to establish (Reid, op. cit., pp. 549–56).

The Conservatives and the voluntary schools

On leaving the Education Department Forster wrote to his sister-in-law:

I do believe some education is now secured to all English children. Whether that *some* is to be enough to be of real value is now the question, but I do not think the work can stop, and I believe Lord Sandon will do his best to carry it (Reid, op. cit., p. 574).

The Conservatives, in fact, were by no means indifferent to social reform, although it had been left 'very much a matter, between 1846 and 1866, of the sporadic efforts of individuals' (Smith, 1967, p. 20) such as Sir John Pakington, the Worcestershire Baronet whose educational work has already been noted, the devoutly Christian C. B. Adderley, former Vice-President of the Council, Staffordshire gentleman and sponsor of the Manchester and Salford Bill in 1854, and Sir Stafford Northcote, protégé of Disraeli and author of the Industrial Schools Bill carried by Adderley in 1857. Despite the presence of such people, however, the Conservatives in the 1860s were still suspicious of popular education, regarding it as potentially subversive of the social order. They nevertheless recognized its value as a palliative, in that it trained the labouring classes to be content with their lowly status. As Disraeli stated in 1862, 'it is the best guarantee of public order' (Moneypenny and Buckle, 1916, iv, p. 379). However, whereas the Liberals and their Radical allies saw education mainly in terms of the urban problem, the Conservatives saw it in rural terms, that is as the inculcation by the clergy of conservative attitudes and sympathies in support of the social and political system of the landed interest. The cardinal point of the party's attitude, therefore, was to maintain the denominational system and the Anglican domination, opposing both an education rate and compulsory attendance; the former in the belief that it would destroy the voluntary schools and the latter on the grounds that it would threaten the rural labour supply.

Forster's bill was welcomed by the Conservatives, particularly by Pakington and Lord Sandon, but by 1874, by which time the latter had become Vice-President of the Council, it had become clear that the voluntary schools were losing in the contest with the rate-supported board schools, being unable to cope with rising costs. As Sir Massey Lopez wrote to Sandon in January 1875:

I am satisfied that the voluntary schools will not be able much longer to hold their own in the rural districts on account of increasing expenses and not able to secure a (proportional) amount of government assistance owing to the attendance of children being so small and so irregular (Smith, op. cit., p. 243).

Under these circumstances it is small wonder that many voluntary school supporters began to recognize in compulsory school attendance a means of survival, in that more children would actually go to school, and, as a result of attending regularly, would be likely to perform better at the annual examination, thereby earning a correspondingly higher exchequer grant. That the problem was largely a rural one is shown by the fact that in 1873, only 40 per cent of the population were affected by the compulsory by-laws, a figure which had risen to 50 per cent by 1876. However, the proportion for the boroughs was as high as 84 per cent, emphasizing the slow progress made in rural areas (Report of the Education Department 1875–6, p. 289).

Lord Sandon, a deeply religious man for whom elementary education was synonymous with Christian education, was determined to rescue the voluntary schools by bringing in a compulsory measure. He was equally determined, moreover, to achieve his objective without creating any more school boards, which to him were nothing less than organs of political subversion, as his memorandum to the Cabinet in 1874 made abundantly clear:

> School Boards (or some such agency) were, I believe, necessary for large towns, and are productive of no political evil, but in the smaller country towns and villages (besides their acknowledged inconveniences) I am convinced they will produce very serious political results. They will become the favourite platform of the dissenting preacher and local agitator and the opportunity for political organization which the politicians of the Birmingham League desire, and which will be mischievous to the State (Smith, op. cit., p. 246).

The voluntary schools, therefore, were to be the custodians of the Tory rural strongholds.

The failure of the Agricultural Children's Act

Sandon was aided in his search for wider support within the Conservative Party by the failure of Read's Agricultural Children's Act. Passed in 1873, its declared objective had been to extend the educational provisions of the factory acts to children working in agriculture, but in the absence of any enforcement agency, an omission illuminated by George Dixon and A. J. Mundella during the bill's passage, it was virtually a dead letter and there is little doubt that its real purpose was to forestall any further extension of school boards in rural areas (Horn, 1974, p. 30).

Further support accrued when the Royal Commission on the Factory and Workshop Acts, established by the Conservatives, reporting in Spring 1876, not only condemned the act as 'doing harm by giving the sanction of state approval to the minimum of school attendance', but also went on to castigate the entire system of indirect compulsion as educationally unsatisfactory. As if this were not enough, Sandon was provided with more ammunition when a deputation, led by no less eminent a personage than the Archbishop of Canterbury, asked for aid to the voluntary schools and an extension of compulsory education.

The activity of the opposition, meanwhile, had given the matter a degree of urgency, for in 1874, 1875 and 1876 George Dixon and A. J. Mundella had introduced bills in support of compulsory attendance and universal school boards, Mundella having told the House in 1875 that out of three million children of school age, 1,400,000 were virtually absentees (Armytage, 1951, p. 101). It was obvious, therefore, that if the Conservatives did not legislate the Liberals eventually would, and that would mean making the dreaded school boards universal. Accordingly Sandon's memorandum of 1876 raised the spectre of a constitution in imminent danger of destruction from the exposure of three or four million children to the subversive influence of 'an army of some 20,000 skilled teachers . . . having received no special religious and moral teaching themselves . . . restless, over-educated, and dissatisfied with their position' (Sutherland, op. cit., p. 136). No doubt he was guilty of exaggeration, but at least the Cabinet were persuaded by his argument.

Lord Sandon's Act, 1876

The resultant bill, however, was half-hearted, being yet another measure of permissive compulsion. It provided for the appointment of school attendance committees in non-school board areas by borough councils in boroughs, boards of guardians in poor law unions and, where they existed, urban sanitary authorities. However, although vested with the right to adopt by-laws enforcing attendance, neither they nor the existing school boards were actually compelled to do so, for as Sandon admitted, 'The Government start from this position. They do not think the principle of direct compulsion would be a good thing itself.' For this Mundella dubbed him 'The mildest-mannered man that ever scuttled a ship or slit a throat' (Armytage, op. cit., p. 167); the ship being the principle of compulsion, and the severed throat that of the Nonconformist body. Nevertheless, as Francis Adams remarked, Sandon's measure was 'an act for compelling attendance in denominational schools supported out of rates and taxes' (Adams, op. cit., p. 319).

The Act put the parent under a legal obligation to send his child to school. If he neglected to do so he could be fined and the child admitted to an industrial school. No child under ten was to be employed, nor any between ten and fourteen unless he or she had passed Standard IV or had made 250 attendances each year for a period of five years – the 'dunce's pass'. Meanwhile, the payment of the fees of poor children under the controversial Clause 25 of the 1870 Act, as proposed earlier by Forster, was transferred to the boards of guardians.

The permissive nature of the Act and its many loop-holes were bound to arouse feelings of irritation not only among the Liberals but also among the more progressive Conservatives. As Hamond, the member for Newcastle-on-Tyne, complained with regard to the provision allowing eight-year-old children to perform agricultural labour for six weeks a year, his colleagues 'were debating this clause as if the object of the Bill were to provide labour for the farmers at the cheapest rate, and not to carry education to the rural districts' (HC, 230, 1420). A further indication of the order of Tory priorities was provided by Sandon's insistence, much to Disraeli's disgust, on the amendment providing for the dissolution of school boards; a measure considered by the Liberals to be an unwarranted assault on the most recent addition to the apparatus of English local government.

For the majority of Conservatives, therefore, improvements in education were secondary to the main priority of preserving the denominational system in rural areas, and compulsion was accepted without enthusiasm in order to keep the school boards at bay. Clearly the Act was not the embodiment of any coherent policy, but merely part of the process of 'empirical piecemeal reform, dealing with problems as and when they were pushed into prominence by their inherent size and urgency . . . by pressure of public opinion . . . and by the exigencies of party politics' (Smith, op. cit., p. 254). It was designed to preserve the supremacy of the Tories in the countryside, and once it was safely on the Statute Book the party's interest in education lapsed.

The Mundella Act, 1880

Lord George Hamilton, Sandon's successor as Vice-President of the Council, was well aware of the deficiencies of the new legislation. Disturbed as he well might be at the activities of the London School Board in providing education beyond the elementary stage, which were to lead in 1900 to the Cockerton Judgment's declaration of their illegality, he was, nevertheless, well disposed toward the newly developing higher-grade schools which provided a quasi secondary education for bright, elementary-school children in the industrial towns. Moreover, convinced of the need for compulsory attendance, he was in the process of formulating a more stringent bill when the government went out of office in 1880, leaving the matter to be completed by his Liberal successor, A. J. Mundella, 'one of the most violent radicals', according to Queen Victoria (Armytage, op. cit., p. 192).

It was fitting that Gladstone should give the Vice-Presidency to Mundella, for no-one could have been more assiduous in bludgeoning the Conservatives into accepting the need for compulsion than the brazen-voiced member for Sheffield. A pioneer of industrial relations, praised by T. H. Green for his work toward limiting the hours of factory labour

(Nettleship, op. cit., iii, p. 369), he embodied the spirit of the New Liberalism which Green did so much to define. Moreover, he saw education as a crucially important element in his grand design for industrial harmony, enabling working men to cope with the complexities of collective bargaining and conciliation machinery which he had pioneered in his Nottingham hosiery factory. Furthermore, his experiences as a juror at the Paris Exhibition of 1878 had convinced him of the need to supplant apprenticeships with a state-provided technical education system capable of training workers for the new science-based industries which were coming increasingly to dominate the industrial scene.

Mundella, meanwhile, was delighted with his appointment, explaining to a friend, 'Nothing could be more gratifying. . . . It has been my life's work and study' (Armytage, op. cit., p. 192). Appropriately, for one of the new breed of Liberals who saw the state as the guarantor rather than the enemy of the liberty of the individual, his first act was to complete the legislation of 1870 and 1876 by ending the farce of permissive compulsion.

Mundella's Act, accordingly, required all authorities which had not made by-laws to do so 'forthwith'. Those which failed to comply by the end of 1880 would be supplied with by-laws framed by the department. In addition, employers of any child between the ages of ten and thirteen were liable to a penalty if that child had not a certificate of education as provided by the by-laws. Full-time attendance was required between the ages of five and ten, and exemption for those between the ages of ten and thirteen could be secured by a standard of proficiency fixed by the by-laws. At thirteen exemption was attainable on attendance alone, and at fourteen the child was free. Even after this piece of elaborate legislation the provisions continued to differ between authorities as to the minimum leaving age. Nevertheless, the basic bureaucratic structure for elementary education had been completed and the nation was now legally obliged to educate its children without exception.

Some indication of the impact of the Act and of the growing power of the central authority can be gained from the fact that before it was passed 450 out of 2000 school boards, twenty out of 190 school attendance committees, and seven out of sixty-seven urban sanitary authorities had not submitted by-laws for approval, and 569 out of 584 unions had not completely covered all their parishes. Within five months of the passing of the Act, over 1200 sets of by-laws were sanctioned, and by 1881 only twenty-eight unions, eighty-one school boards, one school attendance committee and one urban sanitary authority had failed to comply.

The attendance problem did not disappear overnight – in fact it is still with us today. Nor is it likely to disappear so long as schools are expected to perform a custodial role, for there will always be pupils who would prefer to be elsewhere. Nevertheless, in spite of the writing of Ivan Illich (1971) and other advocates of the de-schooled society, it is most unlikely that any industrial society could seriously envisage dispensing with the custodial role of the school. Nineteenth-century England certainly could not. The rural areas, however, continued to present peculiar difficulties even after education had become free in 1891, the problem only being diminished after the end of the century, when mechanization made child labour in agriculture as superfluous as it had already become in the factory.

By 1880 a firm foundation had been provided on which to build an articulated education system. Moreover, before his act was even on the Statute Book, Mundella (Cobden's greatest admirer) had already begun to capitalize on it. His new code broadened the elementary-school curriculum by making subjects such as heat, light, sound, chemistry, cookery and agriculture grant-earning. Furthermore, the addition of an extra standard VII boosted the already developing higher-grade schools in the urban centres of Bradford, Sheffield, Nottingham, Leeds, Manchester, and many others. Like Cobden, Playfair and Prince Albert before him, Mundella viewed these developments as crucial to economic survival, a conclusion which his own experience as a manufacturer, and the publication of his business associate, H. M. Felkin's *Technical Education in a Saxon Town* (1881), caused him inevitably to draw. Felkin's report, in fact, symbolized the British economic problems in face of German competitive energy, describing how the efforts of the local chamber of commerce in the field of technical education had enabled the Saxon town of Chemnitz to challenge the pre-eminence of the Nottingham hosiery trade. The report also provided much of the impetus for setting up the Samuelson Commission, which investigated foreign practice in technical education.

Such problems notwithstanding, by 1881 the economic and social exigencies of an industrialized society had resulted in the establishment of an elementary education system which was universal, compulsory and, as such, symbolic of the new collectivist era which the country was entering. For the education acts were not an isolated phenomenon, but part of a whole body of legislation concerning public health, industry, the protection of the young and the obligation of the individual toward the state. Eighteenth-century philosophers such as Godwin and Priestley might well have argued that the liberty of the individual had been eroded by state intervention. On the other hand, had they been living in the last quarter of the nineteenth century they might equally as well have agreed with T. H. Green that it had been enhanced, as he argued in a lecture delivered in Leicester in 1881, entitled *Liberal Legislation and Freedom of Contract*:

If I have given a true account of that freedom which forms the goal of social effort we shall see that freedom of contract; freedom in all the forms of doing what one will with one's own, is valuable only as a means to an end. The end is what I call freedom in the positive sense; in other words, the liberation of the powers of all men equally for contributions to a common good. . . . Our modern legislation then with reference to labour, and education, and health involving as it does manifold interference with freedom of contract, is justified on the ground that it is the business of the state . . . to maintain the conditions without which a free exercise of the human faculties is impossible (Nettleship, op. cit., pp. 372–4).

Suggestions for further reading

A fascinating and extremely readable account of the economic developments from 1750 to the early 1960s, providing excellent chapters on change in the mid-Victorian period, is E. J. Hobsbawm's *Industry and Empire*, Penguin Books, 1969. Another work, more specific to the period in question, which calls attention to particularly important factors operating in the middle of the nineteenth century, is G. Kitson Clark's *The Making of Victorian England*, Methuen, 1962, while two other very helpful studies are W. L. Burn's *The Age of Equipoise*, Allen & Unwin, 1964, and Geoffrey Best's *Mid-Victorian Britain, 1851–75*, Weidenfeld & Nicolson, 1971.

As for books directly concerned with educational development, Francis Adams's *History of the Elementary School Contest in England* together with A. Briggs's excellent introduction to the recent Harvester Press edition (1972) is essential to the understanding of the motives of radical reformers in the growing industrial towns. Equally indispensable, by reason of the importance of provincial pressure groups in general and Manchester's influence on the 1870 legislation in particular, is S. E. Maltby's *Manchester and the Movement for National Elementary Education, 1800–1870*, Manchester University Press, 1918. Of more recent origin, W. H. G. Armytage's *A. J. Mundella, 1825–1897, The Liberal Background to the Labour Movement*, Benn, 1951, together with his 'W. E. Forster and the Liberal Reformers' in A. V. Judges (ed.), *Pioneers of English Education*, Faber, 1952, and 'The 1870 Education Act', *British Journal of Educational Studies*, xviii, 2 June 1970, are, as always, stimulating and informative contributions.

Meanwhile, Brian Simon's *Studies in the History of Education, 1780–1870*, Lawrence & Wishart, 1960, emphasizing the social-class context of educational development, is a most informative and challenging study. However, if it is the essence of attitudes, hopes and fears of contemporaries which is required, one need go no farther than the National Education Union's Verbatim Report of the debate on the Elementary Education Bill.

Bibliography

The first date of publication is given in all cases. Mention of a later edition indicates the one to which reference is made in the text. The place of publication is London unless otherwise stated.

Official reports, and manuscript sources

House of Commons Debates.

Minutes of the Committee of Council on Education, 1850–1.

Minutes of the Lancashire Public School Association and the National Public School Association. MS deposited in Manchester Central Library at M136.

National Education Union (187Q), *A Verbatim Report, with Indexes of the Debate in Parliament during the Progress of the Elementary Education Bill 1870.*

Report of the Select Committee of the House of Commons on Manchester and Salford Education, 1852–3.

Report of the Oxford University Commission, 1852.

Report of the Cambridge University Commission, 1852.

Annual Report of the National Public School Association, 1854.

Report of the Commissioners appointed to inquire into the State of Popular Education in England (Newcastle Report), 1861.

Report of the Public School Commission (Clarendon Report), 1864.

Report of the Schools Inquiry Commission (Taunton Report), 1868.

Report of the Select Committee on Endowed Schools Act (1869), 1887.

Books, pamphlets and journals

ADAMS, F. (1882), *History of the Elementary School Contest in England*, Brighton, Harvester Press, 1972.

APPLEMAN, P., MADDEN, W. A. and WOLFF, M. (1959), *Entering an Age of Crisis*, Bloomington, Indiana University Press.

84

ARCHER, R. L. (1921), *Secondary Education in the Nineteenth Century*, Cambridge, Cambridge University Press.
ARMYTAGE, W. H. G. (1951), *A. J. Mundella, 1825–1897. The Liberal Background to the Labour Movement*, Ernest Benn.
ARMYTAGE, W. H. G. (1952), 'W. E. Forster and the Liberal Reformers', A. V. Judges (ed.), *Pioneers of English Education*, Faber.
ARMYTAGE, W. H. G. (1957), 'Some Aspects of American Influence on British Education', *Advancement of Science*, 1957, xiii, 301.
ARMYTAGE, W. H. G. (1964), *Four Hundred Years of English Education*, Cambridge, Cambridge University Press.
ARMYTAGE, W. H. G. (1970), 'The 1870 Education Act', *British Journal of Educational Studies*, xviii, 2 June 1970.
ARNOLD, M. (1868), *Schools and Universities on the Continent*, Macmillan.
ASHBY, E., Baron (1963), *Technology and the Academics: An essay on Universities and the Scientific Revolution*, Macmillan.
ASHWORTH, W. (1960), *An Economic History of England, 1870–1939*, Methuen.
BALLS, F. E. (1967), 'The Endowed Schools Act 1869 and the Development of the English Grammar Schools in the Nineteenth Century, i. The Origins of the Act', *Durham Research Review*, v, 19 September 1967.
BALLS, F. E. (1968), 'The Endowed Schools Act 1869 and the Development of the English Grammar Schools in the Nineteenth Century, ii. The Operation of the Act', *Durham Research Review*, v, 20 April 1968.
BAMFORD, T. W. (1967), *Rise of the Public Schools: A study of boys' public boarding schools in England and Wales from 1837 to the present day*, Nelson.
BAXTER, R. DUDLEY (1868), *National Income*, Macmillan.
BINGHAM, J. H. (1949), *The Period of the Sheffield School Board, 1870–1903*, Sheffield, Northend.
BREMNER, J. A. (1867), 'By what means can the impediments to the education of children of the manual-labour class arising from the apathy or poverty of parents and the claims of the market for labour, be most effectually removed', *National Association for the Promotion of Social Science*, Longmans, Green, Reader & Dyer.
BRENNAN, E. J. T. (ed.) (1975), *Education for National Efficiency: the Contribution of Sidney and Beatrice Webb*, Athlone Press.
BRIGGS, A. (1954), *Victorian People*, Odhams.
BRIGGS, A. (1959), *The Age of Improvement, 1783–1867*, Longman.
BRIGGS, A. (1963), *Victorian Cities*, Penguin edition (1968).
BRIGGS, A. (1972), Introduction to Adams, F. (1888), *History of the Elementary School Contest in England*, Brighton, Harvester Press.
BURN, W. L. (1964), *The Age of Equipoise*, Allen & Unwin, 1968 edition.
CARDWELL, D. S. L. (1972), *The Organization of Science in England*, Heinemann.
CAWLEY, E. H. (1952), *The American Diaries of Richard Cobden*, Princeton, New Jersey, Princeton University Press.

Bibliography

CLARK, G. KITSON (1965), *The Making of Victorian England*, Methuen (1962).

CLARK, G. KITSON (1967), *An Expanding Society*, Cambridge, Cambridge University Press.

CONNELL, W. F. (1950), *The Educational Thought and Influence of Matthew Arnold*, Routledge & Kegan Paul.

DICEY, A. V. (1905), *Lectures on the Relations between Law and Public Opinion in England in the Nineteenth Century*, Macmillan, 1926 edition.

Edinburgh Review, December 1831, April 1861.

ENGELS, F. (1845), *The Condition of the Working Class in England*, Panther, 1969 edition.

FARRAR, P. N. (1965), 'American Influence on the Movement for a National System of Elementary Education in England and Wales, 1830–1870', *British Journal of Educational Studies*, xiv, November 1965.

FLETCHER, L. (1972), 'Payment for Means or Payment for Results: Administrative Dilemma of the 1860s', *Journal of Educational Administration and History*, iv, 2 June 1972.

GASH, N. (1953), *Politics in the Age of Peel*, Longmans, Green.

GIFFEN, R. (1889), *The Growth of Capital*, Bell.

GRANT, CAMERON A. (1968), 'A note on "Secular" Education in the Nineteenth Century', *British Journal of Educational Studies*, xvi, 3 October 1968.

HAINES, G. (1959), 'Technology and Liberal Education', in Appleman *et al.*, *Entering an Age of Crisis*, Bloomington, Indiana University Press.

HAMER, D. A. (1968), *John Morley: Liberal Intellectual in Politics*, Clarendon Press.

HANHAM, H. J. (1959), *Elections and Party Management: Politics in the Time of Disraeli and Gladstone*, Longmans.

HARRISON, R. (1965), *Before the Socialists: Studies in Labour and Politics, 1861–1881*, Routledge & Kegan Paul.

HARTWELL, R. M. (1971), *The Industrial Revolution and Economic Growth*, Methuen.

HENNOCK, E. P. (1973), *Fit and Proper Persons: Ideal and Reality in Nineteenth Century Urban Government*, Edward Arnold.

HINTON, J. H. (1852 and 1854), *The Case of the Manchester Educationists*, 2 vols, Manchester, Morten, 1972.

HOOK, W. F. (1846), *On the Means of Rendering more efficient the Education of the People: A letter to the Lord Bishop of St David's*, Murray.

HORN, P. L. R. (1974), 'The Agricultural Children Act of 1873', *History of Education*, iii, 2, Summer 1974.

HURT, J. S. (1971), *Education in Evolution: Church, State, Society and Popular Education*, Paladin, 1972.

ILLICH, I. (1971), *Deschooling Society*, Penguin, 1973.

JONES, D. K. (1967), 'Working-class Education in Nineteenth Century Manchester: The Manchester Free School', *Vocational Aspect*, Spring 1967, xix, no. 42.

KATZ, M. (1968), *The Irony of Early School Reform: Educational Innovation in Mid-Nineteenth Century Massachusetts*, Cambridge, Mass., Harvard University Press.
KATZ, M. (1971), *Class, Bureaucracy and Schools*, New York, Praeger.
KAY, J. (1846), *The Education of the Poor in England and Europe*, Hatchard & Son.
KAY-SHUTTLEWORTH, SIR J. (1862), *Four Periods of Public Education, as reviewed in 1832, 1839, 1846, 1862*, Longman.
LANCASHIRE PUBLIC SCHOOL ASSOCIATION (1847), *A Plan for the Establishment of a General System of Education in the County of Lancaster.*
LANCASHIRE PUBLIC SCHOOL ASSOCIATION (1850), *National Education not necessarily Governmental Sectarian or Irreligious*, Lucas, S. (ed.), Cash.
MACCOBY, S. (1935), *English Radicalism, 1832–1852*, Allen & Unwin.
MacDONAGH, O. (1958), 'The Nineteenth Century Revolution in Government: a Reappraisal', *The Historical Journal*, vol. I, no. i, 1958.
MACK, E. C. (1938–41), *Public Schools and British Opinion: An Examination of the Relationship between Contemporary Ideas and the Evolution of an English Institution*, Methuen.
MALTBY, S. E. (1918), *Manchester and the Movement for National Elementary Education, 1800–1870*, Manchester, Manchester University Press.
McCANN, W. P. (1970), 'Trade Unionists, Artisans and the 1870 Education Act', *British Journal of Educational Studies*, xviii, 2 June 1970.
MILLS, I. PETRIE (1899), *From Tinder-Box to the Larger Light: Threads from the Life of John Mills*, Manchester, Sherratt & Hughes.
MONEYPENNY, W. F. and BUCKLE, G. E. (1910–20), *The Life of Benjamin Disraeli, Earl of Beaconsfield*, 6 vols, Murray.
MORLEY, J. (1873), *The Struggle for National Education*, Chapman & Hall.
MORRIS, N. (1961), 'An Historian's View of Examinations', in Wiseman, S. (ed.), *Examinations and English Education*, Manchester, Manchester University Press.
NETTLESHIP, R. L. (ed.) (1906), *The Works of Thomas Hill Green*, 3 vols, Longmans Green.
PATTISON, M. (1885), *Memoirs*, Fontwell, Centaur Press, 1969.
PERKIN, H. (1969), *The Origins of Modern English Society, 1780–1880*, Routledge & Kegan Paul.
READ, D. (1964), *The English Provinces c. 1760–1960: A study in influence*, Edward Arnold.
READ, D. (1967), *Cobden and Bright: A Victorian Political Partnership*, Edward Arnold.
REID, T. W. (1888), *Life of William Edward Forster*, 2 vols, Chapman & Hall.
ROACH, J. P. C. (1971), *Public Examinations in England, 1850–1900*, Cambridge, Cambridge University Press.
ROGERS, C. D. (1970–1), 'The Case against the School Boards of Cheshire, 1870–1902', *Journal of Chester Archaeological Society*, 57, 1970–1.

ROPER, H. (1973), 'W. E. Forster's Memorandum of 21 October, 1869: A Re-examination', *British Journal of Educational Studies*, xxi, 1 February 1973.

RUBINSTEIN, D. (1969), *School Attendance in London, 1870–1904: A Social History*, Hull, Hull University Press.

SANDERSON, M. (1972), 'Literacy and Social Mobility in the Industrial Revolution in England', *Past and Present*, no. 56, August 1972.

SCHWABE, MME. J. SALIS (1895), *Reminiscences of Richard Cobden*, Fisher Unwin.

SENIOR, N. (1861), *Suggestions on Popular Education*, Murray.

SIMON, B. (1960), *Studies in the History of Education, 1780–1870*, Lawrence & Wishart.

SMITH, F. (1923), *The Life and Work of Sir James Kay-Shuttleworth*, Murray.

SMITH, F. (1931), *A History of English Elementary Education, 1760–1902*, University of London Press.

SMITH, P. (1967), *Disraelian Conservatism and Social Reform*, Routledge & Kegan Paul.

STURT, M. (1967), *Education of the People*, Routledge & Kegan Paul.

SUTHERLAND, G. (1971), *Elementary Education in the Nineteenth Century*, Historical Association.

SUTHERLAND, G. (1973), *Policy-making in Elementary Education, 1870–1895*, Oxford, Oxford University Press.

SYLVESTER, D. W. (1974), *Robert Lowe and Education*, Cambridge, Cambridge University Press.

TAYLOR, A. J. (1972), *Laissez-faire and State Intervention in Nineteenth Century Britain*, Macmillan.

VINCENT, J. (1966), *The Formation of the British Liberal Party 1857–68*, Penguin Books, 1972.

WEST, E. G. (1975), *Education and the Industrial Revolution*, Batsford. *Westminster Review*, VI, 1824.

WILLIAMS, J. N. (1973), 'A Study of the Political Background of the Newcastle Commission 1858–61, and of the Men Appointed to Serve on it', unpublished MEd dissertation in the University of Leicester.

WOODARD, N. (1848), 'A Plea for the Middle Classes', in Roach (1971).

WYSE, SIR T. (1837), 'Education in the United Kingdom', *Central Society of Education*, Woburn Press, 1968.

ZAINU'DDIN, A. (1964), 'England and Australia: National Education in Two Pluralist Societies', in E. L. French (ed.), *Melbourne Studies in Education*, Melbourne, Melbourne University Press.

Students Library of Education

General Editor Lionel Elvin

From College to Classroom: The Probationary Year. Derek Hanson and Margaret Herrington. 128 pp.
The Study of Education. J. W. Tibble. 240 pp.

METHOD

Change in Art Education. Dick Field. 132 pp.
Changing Aims in Religious Education. Edwin Cox. 108 pp.
Children and Learning to Read. Elizabeth J. Goodacre. 128 pp.
Discovery Learning in the Primary School. John Foster. 158 pp.
Environmental Studies. D. G. Watts. 128 pp.
*__The Future of the Sixth Form.__ A. D. C. Peterson. 96 pp.
*__Inspecting and the Inspectorate.__ John Blackie. 112 pp.
*__The Learning of History.__ D. G. Watts. 128 pp.
*__The Middle School Experiment.__ Reese Edwards. 112 pp.
Reading in Primary Schools. Geoffrey R. Roberts. 108 pp.
Spelling: Caught or Taught? Margaret L. Peters. 96 pp.
Students into Teachers: Experiences of Probationers in Schools. Mildred Collins. 112 pp.

HISTORY

*__Advisory Councils and Committees in Education.__ Maurice Kogan and Tim Packwood. 136 pp.
The American Influence on English Education. W. H. G. Armytage. 128 pp.
The Changing Sixth Form in the Twentieth Century. A. D. Edwards. 115 pp.
*__Church, State and Schools in Britain 1800–1970.__ James Murphy. 192 pp.
*__English Education and the Radicals 1780–1850.__ Harold Silver. 148 pp.
*__English Primary Education and the Progressives 1914–1939.__ R. J. W. Selleck. 206 pp.
The Evolution of the Comprehensive School 1926–1972. David Rubinstein and Brian Simon. 148 pp.
The Evolution of the Nursery-Infant School. Nanette Whitbread. 160 pp.

The Foundations of Twentieth-Century Education. E. Eaglesham. 128 pp.

The French Influence on English Education. W. H. G. Armytage. 128 pp.

*The German Influence on English Education. W. H. G. Armytage. 142 pp.

Mediaeval Education and the Reformation. J. Lawson. 128 pp.

Recent Education from Local Sources. Malcolm Seaborne. 128 pp.

*The Russian Influence on English Education. W. H. G. Armytage. 138 pp.

Secondary School Reorganization in England and Wales. Alun Griffiths. 128 pp.

Social Change and the Schools: 1918–1944. Gerald Bernbaum. 128 pp.

The Social Origins of English Education. Joan Simon. 132 pp.

PHILOSOPHY

Education and the Concept of Mental Health. John Wilson. 99 pp.

Indoctrination and Education. I. A. Snook. 128 pp.

Interest and Discipline in Education. P. S. Wilson. 142 pp.

The Logic of Education. P. H. Hirst and R. S. Peters. 196 pp.

Philosophy and the Teacher. Edited by D. I. Lloyd. 180 pp.

The Philosophy of Primary Education. R. F. Dearden. 208 pp.

Plato and Education. Robin Barrow. 96 pp.

Problems in Primary Education. R. F. Dearden. 160 pp.

PSYCHOLOGY

Creativity and Education. Hugh Lytton. 144 pp.

Group Study for Teachers. Elizabeth Richardson. 144 pp.

Human Learning: A Developmental Analysis. H. S. N. McFarland. 136 pp.

An Introduction to Educational Measurement. D. Pidgeon and A. Yates. 122 pp.

Modern Educational Psychology: An Historical Introduction. E. G. S. Evans. 118 pp.

An Outline of Piaget's Developmental Psychology. Ruth M. Beard. 144 pp.

Personality, Learning and Teaching. George D. Handley. 126 pp.

*Teacher Expectations and Pupil Learning. Roy Nash. 128 pp.

Teacher and Pupil: Some Socio-Psychological Aspects. Philip Gammage. 128 pp.

Troublesome Children in Class. Irene E. Caspari. 160 pp.

SOCIOLOGY

Basic Readings in the Sociology of Education. D. F. Swift. 368 pp.
Class, Culture and the Curriculum. Denis Lawton. 140 pp.
Culture, Industrialisation and Education. G. H. Bantock. 108 pp.
*Education at Home and Abroad.** Joseph Lauwerys and Graham
Tayar. 144 pp.
Education, Work and Leisure. Harold Entwistle. 118 pp.
**The Organization of Schooling: A Study of Educational Grouping
Practices.** Alfred Yates. 116 pp.
*Political Education in a Democracy.** Harold Entwistle. 144 pp.
The Role of the Pupil. Barbara Calvert. 160 pp.
The Role of the Teacher. Eric Hoyle. 112 pp.
The Social Context of the School. S. John Eggleston. 128 pp.
The Sociology of Educational Ideas. Julia Evetts. 176 pp.

CURRICULUM STUDIES

*Towards a Compulsory Curriculum.** J. P. White. 122 pp.

INTERDISCIPLINARY STUDIES

*Educational Theory: An Introduction.** T. W. Moore. 116 pp.
Perspectives on Plowden. R. S. Peters. 116 pp.
*The Role of the Head.** Edited by R. S. Peters. 136 pp.

* Library edition only